COMHAIRLE CHONTAE ÁTHA CLIATH THEAS
SOUTH DUBLIN COUNTY LIBRARIES

CASTLETYMON BRANCH LIBRARY
TO RENEW ANY ITEM TEL: 452 4888

Items should be returned on or before the last date below. Fines,
as displayed in the Library, will be charged on overdue items.

THE CELTIC BOOK OF LIVING AND DYING

THE ILLUSTRATED GUIDE TO CELTIC WISDOM

JULIETTE WOOD

dbp

DUNCAN BAIRD PUBLISHERS

LONDON

The Celtic Book of Living and Dying
Juliette Wood

To Robert and Clive

First published in the United Kingdom and Ireland in 2000 by
Duncan Baird Publishers Ltd
Sixth Floor, Castle House
75–76 Wells Street
London W1P 3RE

Conceived, created and designed by Duncan Baird Publishers

Managing Editor: Judy Dean
Editors: Ingrid Court-Jones with Chris Westhorp and Georgina Harris
Designer: Dan Sturges
Picture research: Cee Weston-Baker
Commissioned artwork: Sally Taylor (artistpartners ltd)

British Library Cataloguing-in-Publication Data:
A catalogue record for this book is available from the British Library

1 3 5 7 9 10 8 6 4 2

ISBN: 1-900131-64-1

Typeset in Goudy MT and Goudy Old Style MT
Colour reproduction by Colourscan, Singapore
Printed by Imago, Singapore

NOTE
The abbreviations CE and BCE are used throughout this book:
CE Common Era (the equivalent of AD)
BCE Before the Common Era (the equivalent of BC)

CONTENTS

· · · · · · · · · ·

INTRODUCTION

· · · · · · · · · · ·

Contemporary descendants of the Celts have a reputation for relishing poetry and the wisdom of the imagination. But as a result of changes in language, immigration patterns, and their absorption into larger nations, many people with Celtic ancestors do not speak any of the six Celtic languages (Irish, Manx, Scots-Gaelic, Welsh, Breton and Cornish) in which their heritage is preserved. Not since the days of the Greeks and the Romans has the term "Celtic" been so broadly applied and so hard to define.

Our knowledge of the ancient Celts comes mainly from archaeological research and classical commentaries. Greeks and Romans described the Celts as fearsome but fascinating barbarians, whose bravery they much admired. The authors of antiquity were also intrigued by the ebullience of this colourful people and were fascinated by their religion. It was an outsider's view, certainly, but one that endured down through the centuries, conjuring up romantic images of courageous warriors and heroes, supernatural women and wise druids. Today, we tend to regard the early Celts as singers, poets and outstanding craftsmen who imbued their art and artefacts with a tradition of mystic wisdom that is still very relevant to our times.

In *The Celtic Book of Living and Dying* we explore the key themes of this wisdom – courage, fertility, time, prophecy, destiny and the afterlife, drawing from a wide range of sources. The ancient Celts had

no written language and, for the most part, such knowledge was transmitted in oral form by trained professionals – bards or druids – using elaborate mnemonic devices. Nevertheless some early inscriptions and several texts have survived. And there is an abundance of Celtic wisdom to be found in accounts by the later Christian chroniclers and in the tales and poetry of medieval literature.

The rich heritage of the Celts was first preserved in narrative form by Christian scribes. They wrote down poems praising the deeds of historic rulers and fictional heroes, whose actions embodied the behaviour codes of the people. They documented laws defining important institutions such as kingship and marriage, as well as the position of men, women and children in Celtic society. Gnomic poetry (verse consisting of, or illustrating, a maxim or aphorism) was recorded, which preserved knowledge of the natural world. The scribes also passed down the bardic system of triads (traditional groupings of three associated items), which conserve wisdom in lists of tales, proverbs and general knowledge.

The legacy of their oral and written wisdom tells us much about the spirit of the Celts. Their poems convey powerful, universal sentiments and their narratives tease the listener by intertwining dramatic events with symbolic imagery. Although we may never fully appreciate its original meaning or context, the wisdom tradition encapsulated in *The Celtic Book of Living and Dying* is both thought-provoking and inspiring. Timeless, it is able to strike a chord for many modern readers in much the same way as it may have done for the generations of ancient people themselves.

AN EAGLE'S FLIGHT

A supreme all-seeing eye, the eagle has cosmic associations in many mythologies. Yet the flight of the eagle might also be seen as a metaphor for our own journey through life. In this chapter we trace the human trajectory from childhood, through the duties of Celtic mothers and warriors, to a time when the feasts and triumphs of men and women are no more than ghostly memories, haunting a lonely ruin on a hillside.

THE WISE CHILD

Childhood is a magical time among the Celts. There are laws that codify the duties of parents and foster-parents regarding their young charges' care and education. One of the first responsibilities is to choose a child's name carefully, as the meaning of this name determines its bearer's role in future life. It is also important that a child is named before he or she can be affected by adverse forces that could influence his or her fate. However, many special children – those who possess extraordinary wisdom that they are destined to bring to their people – derive their names from apparent accidents that occur during strange and symbolic adventures in their infancy. Such "wise children" are associated with water at birth or soon after, and undergo a "second birth" from which they emerge precociously knowledgeable, gifted with supernatural powers.

Water is a natural environment for wise children, just as it is the source of vitality for all living things and a symbol for poetic inspiration. The motif of water – as well as those of light coming out of darkness and the psychic gift of "the sight" – recurs in many stories. The young hero Finn, whose name means "shining", dives into water as soon as he is born, to escape the king's attempts to murder him. The child emerges from the water holding a fish, and grows up in secret until he is old enough to claim his heritage. The baby Morfhind, whose name means "great shining", is born in a caul. Because of this he is thrown into the crashing sea to drown but, instead, he surfaces at the ninth wave and begins to speak.

Although wise children start their lives in physical darkness – Morfhind in a caul, the bard Taliesin in a black bag (see below) – they soon acquire names of light that signify the special sight of the poet and seer. The notion that infants possess wisdom from birth (or shortly thereafter) is embodied in the *Book of Taliesin*: "Old is man when he is born and young, young ever after" – a paradox consistent with Celtic belief in the cycle of life, death and the afterlife.

THE SHINING BROW

On Calan Gaeaf – as "Winter's Eve" was known in Wales – Prince Elphin mab Gwyddno, the wastrel son of Gwyddno Longshanks, finds a mysterious black bag in an empty fishing weir. When he looks inside, he finds a child of astonishing beauty. "What a shining brow!" exclaims the prince in Welsh – *tal* ("brow") *iesin* ("shining") – and the wise child immediately takes this phrase as his name. Elphin lifts Taliesin on to his horse and sets off home with him. Elphin's horse instinctively recognizes the special powers of the infant and canters slowly, so that the baby comes to no harm. Prince Elphin becomes so taken with the child that he adopts him to raise as his own son. Taliesin is later to become the greatest of Welsh bards.

THE WARRIOR'S WAY

For the Celts war was not mindless, mechanical slaughter, but a complex craft requiring dedication and skill. In battle a people expressed themselves. According to Julius Caesar, horse-riding warriors known as *equites* were the finest men in Gaul. When the Irish hero Cuchulainn learned to fight, he also learned twenty-seven combat feats with names like "the Apple-Feat", "the Leap-over-Poison" and "the Noise-Feat-of-Nine", which suggest a world of martial arts where discipline and concentration are as important as brute strength. The idea of war as a craft is reflected in the detailed scenes of fighting and the realistic images of warriors practising martial exercises that adorn shields, daggers, swords and spears.

Beautifully decorated weapons, a warrior's most precious possessions, go with him to his grave to serve him in the afterlife. The war-like imagery of the weapons is mirrored in the epithets applied to them by the warriors: "Hundred Battles", "Great Hound", "Serpent with a Terrible Sting", "Proud Boar" and "Rampart of Battle", to name but a few. "Quicker his blood to battle than to feast at a wedding," sings the poet Aneirin (see p.15) of one of these warriors.

Loyalty and bravery are the qualities prized above all, and a wise king knows the value of his soldiers. In the *Gododdin*, an ancient Welsh poem, Aneirin tells of three hundred young men who fight for the king of Gododdin. For a year they accept his hospitality – feasting, drinking mead and receiving costly gifts. These three hundred men are brave, but also clever, courteous to women and accomplished in all the arts, of which war-craft is only one. After a year spent carousing at court, the warriors ride into battle – in the phrase of the poet, "in payment for their mead" – astride white horses given to them by the king, high in spirits and relishing the battle ahead. Although they are all killed, the men die gloriously and their brave deeds are kept alive in song – an immortality on earth to parallel the reward of the afterlife.

THE "WISDOM OF THE SWORD"

Above all, the Celts sought honour in battle – the "wisdom of the sword" – and lived in fear of disgrace. Warriors identified themselves with their personal weapons. As Amergin, one of the great shapeshifters of Irish narrative, declared: "I am the point of a weapon." The best warriors carried the slashing Celtic longsword, and battle poetry praised their skill. Aneirin lauded the men of Gododdin as warriors "who stood firm in battle". At their leader's order, "sword blades descended. They loved combat and bore no disgrace."

Even after their deaths the commander continues to protect his men. For example, Mac Con raises a cairn (a stone burial mound) for each of his companions and they are buried upright with their shields before them, as if their spirits fight on. Warriors' graves are often positioned near rivers or other boundaries so that the dead soldiers constitute a sacred barrier against enemies. When Taliesin and his companion travel through a landscape full of warriors' graves, the poet is asked at each site to name the soldier and give the man's pedigree. That such a powerful seer should be expected to remember the details of dead warriors underlines the high esteem in which the Celts hold their fighting men.

MAGIC WEAPONS

· · · · · · · · · · · ·

As in so many aspects of Celtic life, magic also plays a role in warfare. The hero Cuchulainn has several mysteriously empowered weapons, the most fearsome of which is a barbed javelin. Known as the *gae bolga*, it inflicts multiple, fatal wounds and always returns to its owner of its own accord. Cuchulainn slays many enemies with this weapon. One day he is fighting in the surf against an unknown young warrior.

The two seem evenly matched until Cuchulainn throws the *gae bolga* and mortally wounds his opponent. Only as the victim dies in his arms does Cuchulainn realize he has killed his own son. A supernaturally potent weapon is used by King Arthur's companion, Kei, who helps the king to defeat a monstrous giant. Kei has magic powers and possesses a spear so sharp that it can draw blood from the wind.

The military life is far from being an exclusively male preserve. Warrior women traditionally fight alongside their men or hurl curses at the enemy. War goddesses use magic to transform themselves into fierce battle creatures – and woe betide anyone who offends them. When, before battle, Cuchulainn rejects the amorous advances of a beautiful woman, she reveals herself to be the Morrigan (a dreaded, shapeshifting war goddess) and warns him that she will hinder his fighting. During the battle she attacks him three times, first in the form of an eel, then as a wolf, then as a hornless heifer. Each time the hero wounds her. After the battle she approaches Cuchulainn again and offers the thirsty warrior three drinks of milk – with each one he consumes, one of her wounds heals.

Courage implies the reality and intensity of fear – an emotion the warrior deliberately sought to instil in all his enemies. One Greek writer describes a *carynx*, or animal-headed war trumpet, which Celtic warriors blew before battle to produce an appropriately chilling scream, intended to terrify the opposing ranks. Battle songs, chants and trumpet-blasts produced an appropriate martial ecstasy.

Celtic poets are often fighters as well as singers of songs. Their status as bards gives them special privileges in war so that they seldom perish in the fighting. The poet Aneirin was captured and imprisoned after the battle of Gododdin. Chained up in his cell underground, he sang songs about magic boars and the brave warriors he had known.

The last survivor of the great battle, and the only person who knows how the young heroes had died, Aneirin escapes death so that he might tell of their fate. He composes the *Gododdin*, in which he celebrates the warriors' laughter before they went into the fray, and records their great deeds and glorious deaths so that they will be remembered for ever.

THE HONOUR OF WOMEN

A famous precept of Irish law declares that a woman belongs in the care of her father while she is a girl, of her husband once she becomes a wife, and of her sons after she is widowed. Yet Celtic women are not as passive as this formula might suggest. Classical and Celtic literature alike celebrate women who are true to their sense of honour. Boudicca, the queen of the Iceni (inhabitants of what is now East Anglia), led a revolt against the Romans in 60CE, driving her chariot at the head of the British rebels and seeking vengeance for a just cause. The Roman historian Tacitus depicts her as a red-haired termagant, but he appreciates her loyalty to her tribe and her bravery in taking a stand against the outrages that she and her family had suffered at the hands of marauding Roman soldiers.

In Irish Gaelic literature Deirdre is caught between her love for the handsome Naoise and an impending forced marriage to the old and cruel King Conchobar of Ulster. Furious when his future wife runs away with Naoise and his brothers, Conchobar tricks and kills Deirdre's lover and threatens her with humiliating slavery. She chooses instead to commit suicide, by hurling herself from a chariot and splitting her head open, rather than submit to the wicked king's brutality any longer. Hence she has since often been known as "Deirdre of the Sorrows".

This detail from a Celtic gold collar recalls Blodeuwedd, who plotted with her lover to kill her husband, the semi-divine hero Lleu Llaw Gyffes. Legend has it that she was originally created from flowers. To punish her for her crime, Blodeuwedd was turned into an owl, which was hated by other birds and able to come out only at night. This transformation is apt as the Welsh word for "owl" is "blodeuwedd".

Irish lore commends women who possess a steady tongue, a steady household and steady virtue. These three qualities are explored in the Welsh story of Rhiannon, daughter of an Otherworld king. One day Pwyll, ruler of Dyfed, follows a beautiful woman who is riding a white horse outside his court at Arberth. No matter how quickly he gallops, he is unable to catch her until he addresses her as befits a lady of her rank. The woman reveals to Pwyll that she is Rhiannon, and that she wants him to take her as his wife in order to free her from betrothal to an

THE OLD WOMAN OF BEARE

· · · · · · · · · · ·

In the Irish poem *Cailleach Bheara*, an old woman remembers when she was the mistress of kings. Now she lives alone in Beare with only the wind and sea for company. By turns beautiful and ugly, young and old, she is a symbol of the cycle of life and of the ruler's relationship with the land. In her youthful aspect, she distributes the symbolic cup of rulership, offering female wisdom through the power of water. As an old crone she holds sway over nature – on the Isle of Man she is linked with the weather, and in Scotland she is associated with hunting.

unwanted suitor. Pwyll happily obliges, but at their wedding he is tricked into promising his new bride to the very man she wishes to avoid. Clever Rhiannon intervenes, shows Pwyll how to humiliate his rival, and a year later the wedded couple are reunited.

Once the couple return to Dyfed, Rhiannon soon gains a reputation as the perfect queen. No one leaves the court without a gift from her, reflecting her generous hospitality. However, she is childless, and her husband's foster-brothers begin to spread malicious rumours against her.

When finally a son is born, there is great rejoicing, but the baby disappears mysteriously and the queen is accused of killing her own child. There is blood on her face, but this in fact was smeared there by the women of the watch, who have killed a dog for its blood – they are afraid that their supposed negligence will cost them their lives. Rhiannon maintains a dignified silence in the face of the accusations and throughout her subsequent punishment, never once apportioning blame or protesting her innocence. Her endurance is rewarded when her child is returned alive and well, whereupon she regains her reputation as a good queen and mother – and as a woman of honour.

This rare bronze figure – one of only three Celtic sculptures of dancers ever discovered – was found with other sacred treasures at a Celtic shrine in the Loiret region of France. Thought to be approximately 2,000 years old, the figurine may represent a worshipper or she could be a priestess taking part in a ritual dance to celebrate the festival of a deity. Later Celtic poets praised the grace and beauty of women such as this lithe and graceful dancer, describing them as "cypress shapely" and as having "silken hair, starry like the Milky Way".

A SELFLESS MOTHER

. . . .

According to the *Mabinogion*, the foster-mother who takes in and raises Rhiannon's baby (see opposite) displays exemplary selflessness. First, she tells her husband Teyrnon, who has rescued the child, that she will gladly care for him: "Lord, pleasure and happiness this would be to me if it were your will." Then, when the child's true parentage comes to light, she freely agrees to give up the child to his natural mother: "Three things, Lord, we shall gain thereby. Thanks and favour for freeing Rhiannon from the punishment that she endures. Gratitude from Pwyll for nurturing the boy and restoring him. And the third thing, if the boy becomes a virtuous man, he will be our foster-son and render us all the good in his power." The woman, who is never named, represents the willing sacrifice that any mother will make to ensure the prosperity of her child.

Rhiannon's baby has been stolen by a malevolent spirit (though later rescued by a lord named Teyrnon, and fostered by his wife) – a risk that all mothers face, necessitating constant vigilance over their offspring. Protective magic can help. By tying knots of red ribbon on children's clothing, mothers are able to guard their youngsters against witches. Babies, however, need worldly protection too if they are not to be snatched by the fairies. A fine example of maternal care is Little Dinogad's mother, who kept watch over him as he slept and sang of the good meat and warm skins that his father would bring back from that day's hunting.

LAST THINGS

On an island southwest of Ireland lives the god Donn, Lord of the Dead, to whom all human beings eventually come to pay homage. He is the ancestor god who lies sleeping in a cave, attended by nine maidens whose breath fans the fire under his magic cauldron. Donn's realm extends to the tombs where Celtic warriors and kings are buried alongside their weapons, jewels and feasting vessels – as well as the chariots in which they will travel to the Otherworld to live for eternity.

ANKOU, THE BRETON HERALD OF DEATH

In Brittany, Ankou comes for the souls of those who are about to die. Just as death can strike at any time and in many ways, so too the figure of Ankou has many guises. Sometimes he is a tall, thin man, at others a skeleton carrying a scythe and shading his face with a broad hat. On some occasions he appears on foot, and at other times he travels in a carriage filled with stones that he discards when a new soul enters the coach. It is said that when a sound like the rattle of stones is heard, Ankou is never far behind.

Celtic tradition holds that the most sacred forms of wisdom derive from the world of the ancestors – the realm of the dead. This explains why even the bright sun descends at night into Donn's shadowy kingdom. The sun is the source of all life, and its movement between the world of the living by day and the realm of the dead by night determines the rhythm of time.

Contact between the dead and the living is a commonplace of the Celtic imagination. The land of the dead is a powerful source of arcane knowledge for the living, yet it is always dangerous for them to go there – and they are forbidden to enter this benighted realm before their time. However, temptations to break this prohibition come thick and fast. According to one classical writer, fishermen in Britain are sometimes disturbed by the souls of the dead, calling to them at night to ferry them to a mysterious island – the home of Donn. Anyone who travels to the Otherworld before their death remains eternally young while there, but ages immediately on their return.

Death is a passage to a different sphere of existence, often preceded by signs and premonitions. For example, shortly before he dies, three red-haired riders from Donn appear to King Conaire – tinged red perhaps by the sunset in Donn's westerly homeland. Other portents of death include corpse candles (lights that hover over the doomed person) and the screeching of crows. The harpist David of the White Rock foresaw his own death in a dream. Upon waking, he asked his wife to bring him his harp so that he could play one last song – the harpist's life ebbed away with the dying strains of this beautiful melody.

THIS WAS THE HOUSE

Palaces and great buildings live and die, just like kings and princes. Celtic bards have recognized this in a tradition of poetry that poignantly juxtaposes the ruins of a building with the merriment that once took place there. In the following extract from the *Canu Heledd* (*Songs of Heledd*), an anonymous 9th-century Welsh poem, the death of King Cynddylan is lamented by his sister Heledd.

"Stand aside, maidens, and behold the homeland of Cynddylan.
Now that flames consume the court of Pengwern,
Alas for those still young, who long for their brothers …

With a heavy heart, I wrap the white flesh in a black shroud,
Cynddylan, prince of a hundred armies.

The hall of Cynddylan is dark tonight, without fire, without bed;
I will weep awhile, then I will be silent.

The hall of Cynddylan is dark tonight, without fire, without light;
Except for God, who will ease my cares …

Sad it is to see Cynddylan's hall
Without a roof, without a fire,
My lord is dead and yet I live on … "

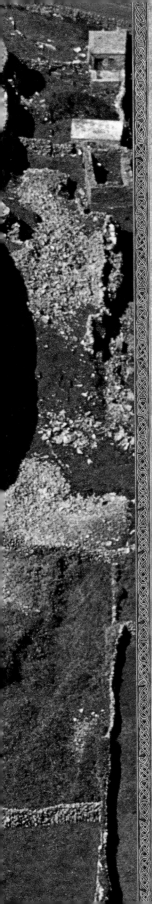

THE
WHEEL OF
NATURE

The Celtic year has no beginning and no end, but follows the rhythms of nature in a continuous cycle. The markers on the calendar are the changes evident in nature. Each new season has a festival that celebrates its agricultural significance. During these festivities, the boundaries between the material and the supernatural worlds are dissolved, and the ghostly inhabitants of the Otherworld break through to enter the realm of the living.

TWO FACES: GROWTH AND DECAY

Nature both gives and takes life, and these two opposite aspects are completely interdependent: nothing can flourish or be healed without destruction. Hence Celtic tradition pairs fierce and powerful animals with gentle goddesses. In mainland Europe bears are watched over by the serene goddess of the forest, Artio, while the boar is looked after by Arduinna, who carries a hunting knife and rides on its back as if it were a tame pony. These deities themselves embody the paradox of life and death in mutual collusion, as they are the patrons of those who hunt the animals as well as of the hunted.

Nature can release its healing strength only by holding its potential for destruction in check through the actions of intermediaries, such as nature gods and their human counterparts, the druids and healers. Some of the physicians to the Scottish kings and lords received their healing powers by eating the flesh of a magic salmon. One Breton tale records how the consumption of a magic snake confers extraordinary abilities, including the power to heal. A young man is lodging with a woman, who is, unbeknown to him, a witch. One day, at her request, he kills a white snake which she puts in a pot to make soup. Feeling hungry, the

This statuette from Berne, Switzerland, portrays a seated female figure with a basket of fruit on a low table next to her. She is offering the food to a bear that is standing in front of a tree. The dedication reads "*Dea Artio*", which means "to the bear goddess" or "to the goddess Artio". The single tree probably represents the forest as a whole. It is likely that this goddess was regarded as both a patron of hunting and the protector of bears, as well as being a deity of the forest.

young man innocently decides to help himself to the brew, and then finds that he has suddenly acquired great powers. He now knows the language of the birds, and how to use magic and to heal with medicinal herbs. He also realizes the true identity of his landlady, and there follows a contest between the witch and the young magician, vying with each other to see whose powers are the greater.

Plants and animals were a source of magic in a world before science sought to explain everything. In one tale, the Irish hero Finn mac Cumhaill touches a salmon that has eaten hazel nuts from trees belonging to the goddess Boinn, and he instantly receives limitless knowledge. Many of the animals and plants from which the ancient healers learned their art also had a religious function. For

PEREDUR'S CHOICE

. . . .

Nature's two-faced aspect is shown in the story of Peredur, whose many adventures were symbolic of his transition from ordinary young man to hero. One day, Peredur saw an extraordinary tree on a riverbank – one side was leafy and green, while the other had flames leaping out from it. Peredur observed the tree and reflected on its symbolism. Near by a young nobleman sat resting. He offered Peredur a choice of three roads. The first road led to a quiet night's sleep, the second to a sumptuous feast and the third to a fearsome monster. Peredur wisely chose the third, which is, of course, the road to heroism.

THE HORNED GOD

· · · · · · · · · · ·

Cernunnos, the "Horned Sacred One", embodies the close relationship between the Celts and the natural world. He is half man and half beast, and is usually depicted sitting cross-legged. Cernunnos has hooves instead of feet, and a pair of antlers sprout from his head, symbolizing the eternal cycle of regeneration.

In some images gold streams from his fingers; or, as here, he holds a snake, another animal alluding to the cycle of renewal. He wears not one, but two torcs – necklaces that denote power and status among the Celts. Cernunnos is god of beasts both wild and tame, and the overlord of nature.

Trees are important symbols in Celtic wisdom – for example, the god Esus is traditionally depicted cutting a willow. With roots that reach deep underground and branches that grow toward the sky, they provide a link between upper and lower worlds. Deciduous trees echo the never-ending cycle of birth, death and rebirth, while evergreens reflect the apparent paradox of eternal life after death.

example, the Roman author Pliny mentions that mistletoe, a plant that was considered particularly sacred by the druids, was used both in a salve to aid healing and as a cure for infertility when mixed in a potion – perhaps because this plant, a parasite, thrives in winter when the host tree appears devoid of life.

In Celtic pagan carvings the god Esus is portrayed as a woodcutter, in the act of cutting a willow tree (illustrated above). The Roman poet Lucan tells us that Esus demanded human sacrifice and that the victims were stabbed, hanged on trees and left to bleed to death. However, Esus, whose name means "Good Master", is often depicted with Cernunnos, the "Horned Sacred One" or "Lord of Animals" (see opposite), which gives us a more sympathetic view of this mysterious deity. In one richly symbolic carving of Esus cutting a branch from a willow tree, the horned nature god is depicted sitting serenely above him on a pillar. Near by is a bull – possibly representing a sacrifice – with three egrets sitting on its back. The birds form a triad (a group of three), which is a recurrent symbol of the sacred in Celtic tradition. Although we do not know what myths the carvings represent, these images combine to suggest nature's power to bring life out of death through the renewal of natural growth in springtime.

THE WISDOM OF
THE WEATHER

In a society dependent on crops and animals for survival, the ability to anticipate the weather accurately is crucial. Celtic folklore abounds with weather maxims – for example, on the Isle of Man, if the sun shines on the hills at the New Year, good fishing is forecast. The following is a selection of anonymous nature poetry, taken from medieval Welsh and Irish manuscripts.

"Falling snow, frost is white;
The wind is strong, the grass freezes;
A shield lies idle on the shoulder of an old man.

Snow falls, covering the ice;
The wind buffets the tips of dense trees;
A shield is splendid on the shoulder of a brave man."
(Welsh)

. . . .

"Mountain snow, the valley is white;
Trees bend under the buffets of the wind;
Many a loving couple never come together.

Mountain snow dapples the air above the tower;
Herds seek shelter;
Unhappy a woman who has a bad husband.

Mountain snow speckles the air before the crag;
Reeds wither, cattle shun the frozen pond;
Unhappy a man who has a bad wife."
(Welsh)

"In the black seasons of midwinter
heavy waves are raised up
along the side of the world's expanse.
Sorrowful are the birds of every plain except the ravens,
that feed on crimson blood.
In fierce winter-time with its uproar,
it is rough, black, dark and smoky."

(Irish)

. . . .

"A mountain storm, rivers in torrents;
Flood water inundates the dwellings;
Everywhere one sees an ocean."

(Welsh)

. . . .

"When the wind is constant from the east,
the energy of the wave is roused:
It wants to go westwards over us,
to the land where the sun sets,
to the broad green ocean."

(Irish)

"Usual is the wind from the north;
Usual is sweetness from a maiden;
Usual is a handsome man from Gwynedd;
Usual is a feast from a prince;
Usual is sadness after drinking.

Usual is wind from the east;
Usual is boasting from a well-fed man;
Usual is a blackbird among thorn bushes;
Usual is much weeping after great violence;
Usual for ravens to eat flesh after a battle."

(Welsh)

· · · · · · · ·

"Outside, rain wets the leaves;
White-caps on the ocean waves; sea-foam on the shore;
Understanding is the light of mankind."

(Welsh)

· · · · · · · ·

"In summer heifers are lowing, weather is brightest, neither bitter
nor wearisome over the lush plain – calm and delightful.
The voice of the wind against the branchy wood, grey with cloud;
the river in spate, the song of the swan, beautiful music."

(Irish)

THE WISDOM
OF THE SEASONS

For the Celts the seasons progress in an ever-repeating cycle, like the turning of a wheel. The sun's power produces life and regulates the cycles of growth of all things, including the crops and animals on which humanity depends.

As natural forces control human destiny, it follows that there are proper times and seasons for all events. At Samhain ("End of Summer"), a festival that takes place every year at the end of October and beginning of November, games are played, stories of heroes are recounted and the people have a chance to enjoy a last, great feast before the onset of winter. It is also a time when the ordinary laws of the world are held in abeyance – spirits can return to the world of the living and the living can travel to the realm of the dead. The Celts believe that Samhain takes place outside ordinary time, allowing fairy mounds to open (see pp.60–61), and humans to have strange, wonderful adventures. Tales of such exploits reflect rituals performed during this sacred period, when mythical and ancestral beings

Fire was an important part of the festivities during both Samhain ("End of Summer") and Beltane ("Bright Fire"). On the night of Samhain household fires had to be covered so that the spirits could not enter and harm the home's inhabitants. Beltane's fires purged the last chill of winter and anticipated the coming of growth, warmth and light. The ashes of these fires were used as a powerful charm against sickness and disease.

SUN AND EARTH

· · · · · · · · · · · ·

The Celtic connection between the Sun and the Earth is expressed in a mythological metaphor depicting a union between a primordial couple: a deity associated with solar power and an earth goddess who is connected with water. The god Sucellos, meaning "Good Striker", holds a double-headed hammer in one hand, blows from which soften the earth (the sun's thawing of frozen ground) and bring forth life. In his other hand he carries a pot to collect the fruits of his labour. This figure was notably popular in wine-growing regions. Accompanying him is the female deity Nantosuelta, whose name means "Stream" and refers to the complementary metaphor of water as the source of life. The seasons turn because of the interplay between these two essential life-giving forces.

are recalled and the spirits are at their most powerful. According to old stories, this is the time when the malevolent Fomorians, a race of monsters, exact their tribute of two-thirds of all the produce of Ireland, and when Aillen mac Midna makes his annual assault on Tara, the Irish court, burning it to the ground (see p.66). That even the gods and heroes of the Celts can defeat these forces only with difficulty makes Samhain a time for reflection as well as for feasting and pleasure.

The next great festival in the Celtic cycle, Imbolc ("the time of milking"), falls at the beginning of February and coincides with the lambing season. For the Celts, then, this is the time to prepare for a new season of farming. After the spread of

THE BLACK SOW

· · · · · · · · · ·

In Celtic tradition the ferocity of boars makes them natural symbols of war, and they also have magical properties and links with the Other-world. Today a black sow still features in an ancient custom that takes place in Wales on Calan Gaeaf, at the start of February. Bonfires are lit on hilltops in every district after dark, accompanied by blowing of horns and dancing. People run past the fire, each throwing a stone into it. When the fire dies down, everyone rushes home to escape the mysterious spirit *Hwch ddu cwta*. As they race away from the dying flames they shout out the rhyme: "Let each try to be first and the tailless black sow take the hindmost." If, on returning next morning, they can find their stone, they will prosper in the coming year.

Christianity, the celebration of Imbolc also became the feast of St Brighid, who watches over farm animals and crops and can control the weather. Her powers are demonstrated in the tale of how, one day, after Brighid had done some laundry, she hung her newly washed clothes on a beam of light, which remained solid until the clothes were dry. The weather at Imbolc is believed to portend conditions later in the season. For example, on the Isle of Man good weather at this time means a bad harvest, whereas bad weather presages a bumper crop. Such paradoxes are one of the most fascinating characteristics of Celtic wisdom.

Beltane, which means "Bright Fire", takes place on Calan Mai (May Day) – the beginning of summer, a time that the poets call "the fairest season". At this festival the Celts built huge bonfires and drove their cattle between them, singing incantations to protect the beasts from disease. Beltane is another time when the

The feast of Imbolc ("the time of milking") at the beginning of February inaugurated the time of raising animals and planting crops. Candles were lit in barns and dairies for luck. Families claiming descent from fairy women believed that if they had brindled (streaked), red-eared or pure white cattle in their herd at Imbolc, the fairies would favour them – they would be assured of prosperity, especially in the dairy.

barriers between the human and spirit worlds come down, but the spirits who visit at this time are gentler than those who come at Samhain. Light overcoming darkness is a dominant theme in the imagery surrounding Beltane, expressed, as so often in Celtic tradition, as a battle between opposites. Gwynn ap Nudd (whose name refers to "light"), a king of the Otherworld, abducted the bride-to-be of Gwythyr ap Gwreidawl. The rivals are condemned to fight each other every Calan Mai until the end of the world, when the winner will finally gain the maiden's hand. Of course, the tale has a poignant dimension, for it is all in vain – at the end of the world the winner will not survive to enjoy the lady's love.

Primarily a festival to honour the harvest, Lughnasa falls at the beginning of August. In Christian times it became known as Lammas. Traditionally, celebrations begin two weeks before the actual day and go on for a further two weeks afterwards. It is a time of feasting and revelry. Games are played – ball games and *fidchell* (a type of Celtic chess) being particularly popular.

Lughnasa is also the personal feast of the god Lugh, who is strongly associated with the agricultural cycle. When the tyrant Balor, king of the Fomorians, learned that his daughter's child would bring about his death, he locked her up in a remote tower. Despite Balor's precautions, the child Lugh was born, and in later life joined the Tuatha De Danann (People of the Goddess Danu), a race of divine warriors, in their battle against Balor. Lugh, a great magician, warrior, harpist, poet and craftsman, was the only one who could kill Balor, whose huge red eye destroyed all that it looked upon, like the scorching sun that parches the crops. The power of Balor's single eye grew as each of its seven coverings was removed – withering, singeing, and finally setting alight everything within its gaze. Lugh eventually put out the eye with a sling shot, thrown with such force that the eye burst out of the back of Balor's head, turning its fatal gaze upon the tyrant's own troops. In this way Lugh tamed the destructive power of nature and protected the harvest. He became king, and prosperity returned after a long age of barrenness.

GWYDION'S ROAD

· · · · · · · · · · · · ·

Like many ancient peoples, the Celts were aware that the earth's seasons reflected movements in the heavens. As well as the Sun and Moon, the Celts also venerated the stars, which were sometimes called the "court of Don" (the Lord of the Dead) and were regarded as important ancestor deities. The most powerful of Don's children was the magician Gwydion. He created a woman from flowers to be his son's wife, but she killed her husband. The grieving father then made the Milky Way as a road to heaven to find his murdered son.

THE SUN AND THE MOON

In a war-torn world, the Sun and the Moon are comforting constants. During the 19th century Alexander Carmichael travelled the Scottish highlands and islands to collect and arrange traditional songs and stories that capture the Celtic spirit.

THE SUN

"Welcome, Sun of the seasons, as you travel high in the skies;
Your steps are strong on the wing of the heights,
You are the glorious mother of the stars.

You lie down in the unending ocean
Without loss and without fear. You rise up on the peaceful wave
Like a young queen in the bloom of beauty.

Glory to you, sun of good fortune.
Glory to you, sun, countenance of the God of the Elements."

THE MOON

"When I see the new moon,
It becomes me to utter my charm;
It becomes me to praise the God of the Elements
For his kindness and his Goodness.

May the moon of moons keep coming through thick clouds,
On me and on every woman –
Coming through black tears.

Seeing how many a man and woman have passed over,
Across the black river of the abyss,
Since last your countenance shone for me, new moon of the heavens."

ECHOES
OF THE
OTHERWORLD

The Celtic Otherworld is a strange, supernatural dimension where the usual laws of time and space do not apply. The Otherworld encompasses the land of the dead, the realm of the gods, the fabled western isles, the kingdom under the sea and the fairy mounds. Humans venture into it at their peril, but those who realize their innate virtues on the quest return endowed with supernatural powers, special knowledge or magic gifts.

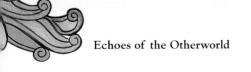

THE ISLANDS BEYOND

The Celts believed in a mysterious island, or a group of islands, which lie to the west, in the direction of the setting sun. Here, the properties of everyday reality are suspended, replaced by a utopian order of heightened possibilities. The characteristics of this utopia vary from one account to another. For example, the birds might sing continuously, the women might be breathtakingly beautiful and people might be immune from aging and mortality.

According to Celtic chroniclers, the one place that remained most elusive to mortal voyagers was a version of the Otherworld called Tir na n-Og – the "Land of Youth". In his description of the monastery on Bardsey Island (just off the coast of North Wales), Gerald of Wales presents a less exaggerated variation of this idea, bringing it closer to a notion of the good life, while at the same time stretching our credulity. Suffering is unknown. The monks live in contentment, apparently dying only of old age and passing on to the afterlife in the order in which they were born, so that the young never die before the old.

The Voyage of Bran, an *imram* story (see pp.68–71) that relates a voyage to the Otherworld, is an appealing example of the more fantastical kind of paradise to which the Celtic imagination responded – one that offers fabulous experiences, but with many snares and delusions to negotiate.

One day a beautiful woman appears at Bran's court and sings to

Crafted entirely from gold, this miniature boat probably represents the type of vessel the Irish Celts imagined voyaging to the Isles of the Blessed. Part of a hoard of precious objects, it may be an offering to a sea deity, such as Manannan mac Lir (see box, p.52), for sailors' protection on a long sea journey.

WISE MEN FROM THE WEST

· · · · · · · · · · ·

A 16th-century Welsh play, written to celebrate the Christian festival of the Epiphany, features the three wise men who brought gifts of gold, myrrh and frankincense to the Christ child. In Christian symbolism the gifts represent kingship, wisdom and power over death – all themes that were also fundamentally important to the Celts. However, there is one significant detail that is changed in the play – the wise men come not from the east but from the west, the mythical land of wisdom and knowledge known as the Otherworld.

him of thrice-fifty distant islands. She refers to one in particular, where sorrow, deceit and death are unknown. Exhorting Bran to set sail for this place, she disappears. Determined to find the special island, Bran puts to sea with three companies, each of nine men. The sailors' first landfall is the Island of Joy, where one of Bran's companions goes ashore. From afar this seems a happy place, but the laughter of the island's inhabitants is mirthless. Once ashore, Bran's companion is unable to return to the boat – he is condemned to stay on the island for ever. The remaining voyagers sail on until they come to a second island – the fabled Island

THE FIN-FOLK OF THE ISLES

· · · · · · · · · · · · ·

On certain islands in the stormy seas surrounding Scotland live the fin-folk. These strange beings, who are not quite mermaids and not quite humans, possess the power of second sight.

Sometimes the fin-folk invite human friends to visit their isles, which have prosperous farms with many cattle. At other times they are caught in fishermen's nets and brought ashore, where they take up residence among humans. Because they can foresee human fate, the fin-folk cry at births and christenings and laugh at funerals.

However, they do not stay long among their alien hosts, often returning home with the help of fishermen. As they approach home, they call to their kin of their impending arrival. After such missions of rehabilitation, the fishermen who take them there are never able to find the islands again.

of Women. One of the women calls out a welcome and throws to the ship a ball of thread, which magically attaches itself to Bran's hand and allows her to pull the ship to the shore. She turns out to be the woman who has previously extolled the pleasures of the island at Bran's court, and her motive for enticing him is love. Bran and the fairy woman become lovers, and he and his men live contentedly here for many years. The land fulfils all the men's desires – beautiful women, soft beds, never-ending food, perpetual summer, a splendid palace and every luxury they could imagine. But finally one man becomes homesick and the voyagers decide to return. Bran's Otherworld mistress begs him to stay but he refuses. Seeing that his mind is made up, the mistress abandons her attempt at persuasion, but warns him against setting foot again on Irish soil. Bran and his men set sail.

When they approach Ireland, the homecoming wanderers call out to the people lining the shore that Bran, son of Febal, has returned. But the onlookers remember no such name, although they do recall an ancient story of "Bran's rowing". The homesick man is overjoyed to be back and he leaps ashore. However, as soon as his feet touch land he disintegrates into ashes. Bran then understands the true meaning of his mistress's warning. From the safety of his craft, he tells the assembly of the voyagers' experiences. Then Bran and his remaining companions set sail once more – and to this day they have never been seen again.

When Bran recounted the tales of his travels (see above) he also wrote them down in a script called "ogham", so that the wisdom gained by his voyage would never be lost. Ogham is the earliest Celtic script, dating from the 4th and 5th centuries CE. Inscribed on standing stones in many parts of Ireland, Scotland, the Isle of Man and Wales, it uses a system of notches and grooves to indicate letters. Although based on the Latin alphabet, ogham was believed to be the magic writing of the druids.

IMPOSSIBILITIES

Young men seeking marriage with a high-born or supernatural bride can expect to rely solely upon their own merits: often, they are required to perform apparently impossible tasks in the Otherworld. Such assignments are not necessarily beyond them, provided that they can show intelligence, resourcefulness and courage, as the following tales illustrate.

In the Otherworld, Ysbaddaden, the chief giant, has a beautiful daughter. The young hero Culhwch wishes to win the girl's hand, but in order to do so he must first succeed in a series of seemingly impossible tasks set by Ysbaddaden. Luckily, Culhwch has many willing helpers with a wide range of talents. One task is to have his bride's wedding veil made – but it must be spun only from flax gathered from a certain field, before the end of a particular day. A colony of ants, whose anthill was saved from burning by one of Culhwch's companions, comes to the hero's aid. When it seems that all is lost and that time will run out before the task can be completed, a lame little ant saves the day by limping in with the last stalk before nightfall.

In another story, an impoverished young man asks to marry the king of Ireland's daughter, who is already promised to a cowardly prince. The king agrees, provided that the suitor can enter the Otherworld and make the miserable *grua-gach* (ogre) laugh again – an ostensibly impossible task that the king believes will save his daughter from marrying beneath her. The suitor enters the ogre's service as a cowherd and, one day, cuts off the heads of three giants who try to steal the cows. The grateful *gruagach* tells the youth how, once, he and his twelve sons spent a night in a giant's castle. When the giant offered them wooden or iron cutlery, they chose the iron and were given no food. Later, offered iron hoops or wooden ones, they chose the iron again. This time the giant strangled the sons with the metal hoops and then cut off their heads. Since that day the ogre has never

laughed. After hearing this sad tale, the young man goes to the giant's castle, where he is asked to make the same choices. He opts for wood, forcing the giant to restore the ogre's sons to life. As soon as he sees his boys, the delighted ogre laughs aloud. The young man returns to the king with news of his accomplishment. Realizing that a brave pauper is a worthier husband for a princess than a cowardly prince, the king lets the young couple marry – he has learned a moral lesson (reflected in the tale by the choice of the apparently inferior material, wood).

JASCONIUS THE WHALE

Among the many amazing adventures that occur during the voyage of St Brendan (see p.71) and his monks is an encounter with a sea creature called Jasconius. The monks land on an island where they collect wood for a fire. Soon, however, the island begins to shiver and shake, and the terrified holy men clamber back into their boat. Unknowingly they have disturbed the whale Jasconius, who has been dozing on the surface of the ocean for so long that plants have grown on his back. St Brendan calms the beast with a discourse on the nature of heaven and earth, and Jasconius graciously acknowledges the power of God before diving into the depths of the ocean, leaving the monks to continue on their journey unharmed.

VEILS OF ILLUSION

To gain access to the Otherworld, travellers have to pass through the veil of every-day reality into the strange beyond. Sometimes this veil is a mist or portal at the entrance to a cave; sometimes it is the surface of the ocean, beneath which lies a wonderful land (see p.52). This theme of things being other than they appear runs through the Otherworld like a seam of silver in a rock-face. Illusions are every-where, and present a major hazard. Sometimes the supernatural world triumphs, the illusions turn out to be snares and travellers do not return; sometimes they return safely, even bringing back a precious object with magic properties.

One common form of Otherworldly illusion is shapeshifting, which in many stories takes the form of the grotesque truth finally shaking off its borrowed finery. Once, a young nobleman fell in love with a beautiful lady, Melusine, who agreed to marry him on one condition – that he never watch her bathe. Their marriage was blessed with many children, but one day the man could no longer resist and spied on Melusine in her bath. Horrified, he saw that his beautiful wife had turned into a sea serpent with small, scaly wings and a tail. Sensing that she had been discovered, Melusine screamed and flew away. Her husband never saw her again, but the children's nurses reported that a ghostly figure with a serpent's tail hovered near their bedsides every night. To this day the cries of Melusine are sometimes heard before a death in the family.

Shapeshifting can also be the instrument of a moral test, as shown in a tale about Annwn, the Welsh Otherworld. Pwyll, the young ruler of Dyfed, is asked by Arawn, king of Annwn, to help him slay a monster which can only be killed by a brave, clever human. To achieve this they impersonate each other. Arawn takes on Pwyll's appearance (so that the people of Dyfed will not know that their lord is absent), ruling the land wisely while he is away. And, in the shape of the Otherworld king, Pwyll goes to Annwn to take up residence with the beautiful

queen. She, of course, believes Pwyll to be her husband, but out of loyalty to Arawn, Pwyll tactfully refuses her advances. He then shows great courage and slays the monster. When the two rulers revert to their real identities, Arawn realizes the true extent of Pwyll's bravery and friendship and rewards Pwyll by giving him the title "head of Annwn".

Pwyll, who might have benefited from supernatural illusion, resists the temptations that come his way. Similar strength of character is shown by St Collen in the following tale. The sinister ruler Gwynn ap Nudd invites the saint to his realm

THE GUARDIAN AT THE WELL

· · · · · · · · · · · ·

Lost in the middle of a forest, Niall of the Nine Hostages and his elder brothers decide to cook the game they have killed. The eldest brother goes in search of water. In due course he finds a well where he meets an old hag who demands a kiss in exchange for the clean, sweet water over which she stands guard. Unable to bring himself to pay such a price, the eldest brother returns empty-handed. Each brother in turn goes to the well and rejects the hag's bargain, until only Niall remains. Unlike his brothers, Niall is content to kiss the hag. His act transforms her into a beautiful young woman, who tells him that her name is Sovereignty and that one day he will be High King of Tara. A true king is able to see that beauty lies within.

Manannan mac Lir
and the Land Under the Waves

. . . .

Manannan mac Lir, the god of the sea, moves easily through his watery realm, his chariot crossing the waves as if it were a field of wheat. His favourite steed is named Enbarr, meaning "sea foam". However, poets call the white-tipped waves "the locks of Manannan's wife". When Bran, son of Febal, was on his sea voyage, Manannan greeted him and told him that beneath his coracle, invisible to mortal eyes, lay Mag Mell – a land of flowers, woods and luscious fruit.

He tells Bran how he has given magic gifts from his Otherworld realm to the Tuatha De Dannan. The gifts included a "coat of semblance" which made the wearer invisible, swine that came back to life each time they were slaughtered and eaten, and "the feast of Goibhniu", which kept the people forever young.

When she bathes, the shapeshifter Melusine (see p.50) becomes a sea serpent from the waist down, with a scaly tail ending in fins. Her scales might be imagined sparkling with the same iridescent properties displayed in this Celtic enamel brooch of a seahorse (1st century CE). The Welsh word for this silvery blue is *glas*, which covers the whole spectrum of shimmering blue shades that appear when a salmon flashes in a stream or when sunlight spears into water.

beneath Glastonbury Tor and asks him what he thinks of the splendid hall shimmering with jewels and the tables laden with delicious food. The saint, however, is not fooled by such an ostentatious display of riches. He sprinkles Gwynn ap Nudd's hall with holy water and reveals the trickster's court to be just a few humps of grass-covered earth.

Some humans find it impossible to resist the riches that the supernatural world can promise. One night a well-dressed gentleman appears at a midwife's door, asking for help because his wife is in labour. Together the man and the midwife ride swiftly through the darkness until they reach a magnificent hall where a woman is giving birth. The midwife soon realizes that this is no ordinary place and that the baby is a fairy baby. But as the fairies often call upon human midwives to deliver their children and reward them handsomely, the midwife is unperturbed. After the birth, the father asks her to rub a special ointment on the infant, but, while performing this task, she touches her own eye by accident. Suddenly the fine hall changes into a dank cave, but the woman says nothing and leaves with her reward. On unexpectedly meeting the man again, she asks after the mother and baby. The man replies courteously but then enquires how it is that she can see him. Rashly, she points to the anointed eye, prompting him to put out the eye so that she can never again see fairies.

MYSTICAL CREATURES

More than just a source of food, clothing and transport, animals had an intense spiritual significance for the Celts. Many creatures were thought to possess supernatural powers or special wisdom, and to be able to move freely between the everyday realm and the Otherworld.

In Celtic folklore, while the boar is often the symbol of the hero, it is the flesh of the pig that provides the hero's food. In many Otherworld feasts swine are killed and eaten, only to come back to life again, providing a never-ending supply of food. Disputes over such magic pigs can have terrible consequences. Arawn, king of Annwn, gives several of them to Pwyll of Dyfed as a reward for his services in defeating a monster (see pp.50–51). The care of these animals passes to Pwyll's son Pryderi. When the magician Gwydion requests them as a gift, Pryderi finds himself in a quandary: should he surrender the creatures to Gwydion, or would this offend Arawn? To persuade Pryderi to give up the pigs, wily Gwydion conjures up hounds and horses to exchange for them. Pryderi agrees to the deal, but the outcome is disastrous: Gwydion's gifts turn back into the grass, mushrooms, flotsam and jetsam from which, deviously, they were created. Pryderi then declares war on Gwydion's family.

The loyalty of dogs makes them the most beloved of domestic animals, but they are also healing symbols, and they are often associated with the Otherworld. King Arthur's dog, Cabell, as big as a horse, left his footprint in a rock, which was placed on top of a cairn. If anyone takes the stone away during the day it magically reappears on top of the cairn by morning.

THE HUNTING OF TWRCH TRWYTH

In the Welsh tale of *Culhwch and Olwen*, the king's armies assemble to hunt down Twrch Trwyth, a boar (once a king) that has stolen a talismanic comb and shears. They find the boar and his seven pig companions in Ireland. Arthur and his men pursue the swine across the sea to Wales, harrying them until only Twrch Trwyth is left. They chase him to Cornwall, where they finally succeed in recapturing the magic implements, and drive the boar into the sea.

Like pigs and boars, stags are associated with heroes, and they also serve as messengers or decoys from the Otherworld. To enlist Pwyll's help, King Arawn sends his hounds to hunt an Otherworld stag on a day when Pwyll is also out hunting. When Pwyll's dogs start to chase a stag through the woods of Glyn Cuch, their master follows and comes upon Arawn's royal hunting party. In this way the Otherworld stag brings the two rulers together.

The nature god Cernunnos (see p.28) has a stag's horns, and the stag is his frequent companion. He represents the eternal cycle of nature manifested in the

seasonal shedding and regrowth of antlers. The symbolism of the stag survived the Celts' conversion to Christianity: in medieval manuscripts the regenerative symbolism of the creature was converted to a metaphor for the death and resurrection of Christ.

Because they shed their skins, snakes, too, are linked with regeneration. Cernunnos is often depicted holding a snake. This creature is also associated with the acquisition of Otherworld knowledge. Not until Christian times do more negative associations begin to appear. For example, the Welsh chronicler Walter Map tells of a hermit who found a little snake outside his cell one morning. The holy

THE DEER'S SON

Oisin, the son of Finn mac Cumhaill, is one of the most important Irish heroes. His name means "little fawn". There are different accounts of his conception and birth. In one version his mother is an Otherworld woman who comes to visit Finn in the form of a doe so that she can lure him into the forest to seduce him. But in another version of the tale, Finn's wife is Oisin's mother. One day while her husband is away, an evil magician turns her into a doe. She flees into the forest where she gives birth to a human baby. Several years later when Finn is out hunting in the same forest, his hounds catch the scent of a deer. When Finn tracks it down, he finds a little boy who says that he has been raised by these animals. Finn recognizes the boy as the child of his lost wife, and names him Oisin.

man takes pity on the creature and gives it milk to drink. He keeps it in his care, offering it food and shelter as if it were a pet. However, the snake grows so big that its coils threaten to destroy the hermit's cell. Finally, the holy man prays to God for assistance, and the huge creature returns to the lake it came from. God has answered the hermit's prayer as a reward for his kindness.

One of the most revered animals is the horse. Often shown pulling Celtic war chariots, horses are much admired for their grace, as well as for their strength. The character of the horse (hardworking and gentle) is highly prized. In order not to break a stallion's spirit during taming, a druid would recite a secret spell into his right hand and then "rub" it on the animal's rump.

Horses often accompany their masters to the Otherworld. Some princely burial mounds include horses complete with their reins and harnesses, ready for their owners' posthumous journey. One of the most famous partnerships of a hero and his supernatural horse is that of Cuchulainn and the "Grey of Macha". The animal emerges mysteriously from a lake, proud and untameable, but Cuchulainn rides it across Ireland all day before bringing it home with him at night. This faithful steed serves the hero all his life. When the omens indicate that Cuchulainn is about to fight his last battle, the horse tries to resist being harnessed to the hero's chariot and weeps tears of blood.

Other animals are associated with magic and divination. Julius Caesar, commenting on the sacredness to the Celts of the cockerel, the goose and the hare, observes that none of these creatures was eaten, because of their sacred associations. The path that a hare follows after being released from captivity is a means of predicting the outcome of an impending battle. With a similar tradition in mind, before fighting the massed Roman forces near Colchester in 60CE, Boudicca, fierce queen of the Iceni, released a hare as an offering to the tribal goddess Andraste. The goddess seems to have answered the prayers of her people that day, because the Iceni gained a great victory over their foe.

TALISMANS OF POWER

Many Celtic stories tell us of precious objects with magical powers, and these may have provided the inspiration for some of the most stunning works of Celtic craftsmanship. Perhaps beauty itself was believed to be part of the supernatural. Finely wrought talismans of various shapes and sizes feature in countless tales of danger and adventure, especially raids into the Otherworld with the aim of capturing them. However, those who covet an object of beauty should beware: in most cases only the good and the true can benefit from its power, and those who are wily or devious will in the end find only discontent. The magician Merlin is said to have hoarded thirteen talismans of power – a catalogue of their special properties and the names of their original owners is found in poetic recitations (see opposite).

One of the best-known talismans is the mighty sword Excalibur, which is given to Britain's monarch, King Arthur, by the magical Lady of the Lake. The sword's beautiful scabbard prevents the wearer from losing blood during battle, and according to the medieval Welsh tale *The Dream of Rhonabwy*, the hilt of Excalibur is engraved with a pair of serpents from whose jaws jets of fire appear to spout when the weapon is unsheathed.

Even with the introduction of Christianity, the talisman remained a prominent instrument of power in Celtic wisdom. With typical pragmatism, poets and bards tell how artefacts that had previously possessed magical, pagan properties have now acquired miraculous saintly efficacy. For example, many Celtic saints were said to carry an iron bell, which after the saint's death was usually kept in a shrine decorated with precious jewels in an intricate design. The bell itself, representing the extraordinary abilities of the saint who carried it, has the capacity to administer life or death – on the one hand curing illness or even bringing the dead back to life; on the other, in the wrong hands, having the power to kill.

MERLIN'S HOARD

· · · · · · · · · · ·

The following are the Treasures of the Isle of Britain kept by Merlin.

White-hilt, the Sword of Rydderch the Generous which bursts into flame from hilt to tip if a well-born man draws it.

The Drinking Horn of Bran of the North which will supply the drink of any man's desire.

The Cauldron of Diwrnach the Giant which will not boil meat for a coward.

The Coat of Padarn Red-coat which will only fit a well-born man.

The Mantle of Tegau Golden Breast which will reach the ground in perfect folds only when worn by a woman of perfect virtue.

The Game of Gwyddbwyll which belonged to Gwenddolau son of Ceidio (and is similar to the modern game of chess). When the game is set up, the silver pieces will play upon the golden board by themselves.

The Hamper of Gwyddno Long Shank which, when food for one is put into it, will provide food for a hundred.

The Chair of Morgan the Wealthy which will transport a man who sits on it to whatever destination he wishes.

The Whetstone of Tudwal Tudgyd which sharpens the sword of a brave man but blunts the sword of a coward.

The Halter of Cludno Eiddyn which will provide a man with any horse he desires.

The Knife of Llawfrodedd the Knight which will serve two dozen knights at table.

The Dish of Rhygenydd the Cleric which provides whatever food one most desires.

Eluned's Ring which the countess Eluned gave to Owain ap Urien. It makes the wearer invisible.

FAIRY MOUNDS

More than all other entrances to the Otherworld, fairy mounds are the most mysterious. Known as *sidh* (pronounced "shee") mounds, they are the ancient tombs of the Celtic landscape. From them fairies emerge to kidnap good-looking men and women, stealing them away to the Otherworld realm where pain and suffering are unknown, and music and feasting the perennial occupations. On moonlit nights in open spaces mortal captives may be seen dancing with fairies, or riding with them on horseback. After dark during Beltane or Samhain the fairy spirits are abroad, and people are able to rescue their loved ones as a fairy procession passes a crossroads. Alternatively, breaking the circle of a fairy dance with an iron knife sends the fairies scattering in fear, enabling the captives to be freed. Any rescues must take place within a year and a day of the kidnapping – those who have spent too long in the fairy world turn to dust as soon as they eat human food again. People have become poets, prophets and seers through fairy kidnappings, although some mortals return with no noticeable effects at all.

Mounds can also be the dwelling places of ancient Celtic deities. The powerful Dagda resides in the great tomb site at Newgrange in Ireland, and Gwynn ap Nudd, a lord of the Otherworld, lives beneath the mound of Glastonbury Tor in southern England. These mounds are also the sacred gateways through which the departed pass on their journey to the Otherworld. The spirits of the dead remain in the mounds for a transitional period to prepare themselves for their onward journey. On certain nights of the year (see pp.34–39), the living, the dead and gods alike can move freely between worlds, using the mounds as entrances and exits.

Only people who are brave or kind are able to remain happily in the Otherworld. One day Fiachna mac Retach, lord of a *sidh*, requests an earthly champion to fight an Otherworld opponent. Loegaire comes forward and defeats Fiachna's enemy. As a reward, Fiachna makes Loegaire joint ruler of the *sidh*

realm. Loegaire marries Fiachna's daughter, Der Greine (whose name means "tear of the sun"), symbolizing the union between the two worlds. Loegaire can pass freely between the mortal and fairy realms, but ultimately he must choose whether to return to the land of the living or stay with the fairies for ever. He chooses the *sidh* world and visits Ireland to say farewell. When his father tries to persuade him to stay, Loegaire's refusal takes the form of a long poem in which he avers, "One night of the nights of the *sidh* is worth an earthly kingdom." He says his goodbyes and is never seen again in the world of the living.

DARK NIGHTS OF THE TOMB

Classical writers marvelled that Celtic poets would spend the night near the tombs of their famous ancestors. Bedd Taliesin, the grave of the famous Welsh bard and prophet, is an ancient tomb overlooking the Dovey estuary in Wales. Anyone who sleeps overnight on the poet's tomb will awaken the next morning as either a poet or a madman. The Celts regarded darkness as the fount of all knowledge, and the dim interior of the tomb, reinforced by the blackness of night, was considered to be an especially magical combination.

VOYAGES
BETWEEN
REALMS

The progress we make from innocence to knowledge or from vengeance to forgiveness is reflected in the journeys of heroes who set out on missions of revenge or rescue, among other tasks, eventually discovering profound truths in the lands beyond. These are odysseys of the imagination as well as voyages into the self. In this chapter we follow several such epic quests, as well as travels between material and spiritual worlds.

THE THRESHOLD OF THE BEYOND

Spirits often enter the land of the living, and conversely, to maintain a balance between the two worlds, humans must sometimes journey to the Otherworld. There are many ways by which the living can reach the spirit realms and one of the most direct means is to cross the threshold where the land of mortals and the kingdoms of the supernatural meet or intersect. Such portals are found both at the centre and at the outer limits of the Celtic world.

The Celtic cosmos radiates from a point where the human and the supernatural domains converge. Julius Caesar tells us that at a certain time of the year the druids met at a spot in mid-Gaul which represents just such a point. The location might have been a sacred grove – one of the dark places where druids held their ceremonies and carried out sacrifices to propitiate the gods and learn the future. Or it might have been an open area, such as the Plain of Tara, in whose centre stands the magic Stone of Fal, which shouts out for the real king.

The vision of highly centralized cosmic order is reflected in the way in which the four outer provinces of ancient Ireland – Connacht, Leinster, Munster and Ulster – extend from the mid-point of Tara in the central province of Meath (roughly the modern counties of Meath and Westmeath). As if to echo this pattern, at the Feast of Tara the kings of the four provinces sit before and behind the High King, and to his left and right, thus surrounding him with the safety offered by Ireland and its formidable warriors.

The tension between cosmos and chaos is analogous to an ancient form of chess. In the centre of the Plain of Tara stand the king and his men, like pieces commanding the middle of the board. All around them are hostile forces. Just as an experienced player can triumph in the game through a combination of skill and

THE WASHER AT THE FORD

· · · · · · · · · ·

Sometimes before battle a beautiful woman from the Otherworld is seen at a river ford, cleaning the clothes of those about to die. One day King Owein Gwynedd saw such a woman, and his dogs howled ferociously. Putting down her washing, she approached him. She explained that she was condemned to wash at the crossing until she had a child by a mortal king. The king freed her from the curse and named the place the "Ford of the Barking" after the dogs who sensed her fairy presence.

luck, so humans can survive their encounters with the supernatural by trusting in both their own abilities and in destiny.

The natural places where the human realm and the Otherworld meet have clear topographical features. Boundaries such as rivers divide them, while lakes and wells act as entrances and exits. Man-made structures such as the walls of forts can be stormed by supernatural as well as mortal attackers. Conn, High King of Tara, patrols the ramparts of his fort daily, standing guard lest the fairy people of the *sidh* ("fairy mound") should creep in and take him unawares.

A love of beauty led the Celts to depict their wisdom in art. Here, the four lines extending outward from a small circle in the middle of this representation of a spoon-shaped object are thought to denote the four outer provinces of Ireland: Connacht, Leinster, Munster and Ulster – with Tara, the royal court, at its centre in Meath. Another interpretation suggests that the decoration may be symbolic of the High King's feasts, where the lesser kings and nobles sat in formal ranks to his north, south, east and west. The exact use of such implements remains a mystery.

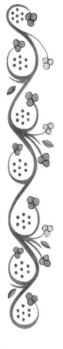

Barriers and doorways between the worlds, both natural and artificial, are more vulnerable at certain times of year (see pp.34–39). The Feast of Tara took place at the festival of Samhain, which was also when Aillen mac Midna, enemy of the Tuatha De Danann, came from the Otherworld to burn down the royal seat. Every year for nine years he had terrorized Tara by lulling the court to sleep with his magic music and then razing the palace to the ground with his fiery breath. At last the High King of Tara asked for volunteers to challenge Aillen, and the hero Finn mac Cumhaill stepped forward. Finn offered to stand guard all night in return for the granting of a wish. The High King accepted and Finn was given a magic spear to enable him to resist the sleep-inducing melody and kill the assailant. When Aillen came, Finn duly vanquished him with the spear and his wish – to become the leader of the Fianna, the elite warband of Ireland – was fulfilled.

On spirit nights many cautious humans stay at home with their doors and windows bolted, afraid of any contact with the supernatural and fearful that the fairies may kidnap them. But the more adventurous, such as Nera, a servant of Ailill of Connacht, whose story is told opposite, might take the opportunity to enter the Otherworld and learn wisdom from the dead. Other human travellers set out on ocean voyages (see pp.68–71) with the intention of reaching the legendary Otherworld islands that lie to the west.

NERA AND THE DEAD MAN

· · · · · · · · · ·

On Samhain's eve at the royal palace of Cruachan, Nera, responding to a challenge from the king, plucked up the courage to approach a dead man hanging at the crossroads. The dead man asked Nera to help him quench his thirst. Being dead, he could only enter a dwelling where there was free access to fire and water. In the first house they approached, the hearth was covered so they could not enter. In the second house the water vessels were empty. But the third house had an uncovered fire and the water vessels were full – so here the dead man could drink. He then instructed Nera to enter the Otherworld through a *sidh* mound. As a reward for helping the dead man, Nera found he could see into the future, and realized that the *sidh* people planned a raid on Cruachan. He returned home, carrying out-of-season flowers as proof of his Otherworld adventure, and informed the king. Thus the raid by the people of the *sidh* was thwarted.

THE ENCHANTED ARCHIPELAGO

The Atlantic Ocean was a formidable proposition even for such intrepid wanderers as the Celts. Nevertheless, Celtic sailors ventured on the open seas in seaworthy *curraghs* – wooden-framed boats covered with waterproofed hides. In the narrative genre known as the *imram*, which literally means "rowing", probable details from actual journeys of exploration are interwoven with fantastical travellers' tales and beliefs about the afterlife to spin richly intricate fables which are characteristic of the Irish Celts.

All the *imrama* stories follow a similar pattern. A group of men embark upon a sea voyage, usually for one of three reasons. They may set out to find the mystical Isles of the Blessed – a group of Otherworld islands that lie "to the west". Or their journey may be penance for having violated a *geas* – a curse that requires the men to complete a series of tasks before the spell is lifted. Or their motive for the voyage may be to seek revenge for a wrong they have suffered – as in the story of Mael Duin, whose encounters include the two islands described opposite. Forming their own Celtic Book of Living and Dying, the *imrama* tales take the voyagers on a series of adventures, each of which provides a special opportunity for learning. Each island has its own peculiar property. On some islands eating the fruit or drinking from the fountains can kill, cure or cause strange transformations. On others the inhabitants obsessively perform a single activity. The laws of nature are no longer guaranteed to operate – for example, monsters might appear from the deep, the sea congeal or come alive, or fish rise from rivers and lakes to speak to the human voyagers.

Such freakish encounters abound in the Mael Duin story. The hero sails from Ireland with warriors and his three foster-brothers in search of the wicked men

TWO LANDS VISITED BY MAEL DUIN

· · · · · · · · · · ·

The Island of Black and White has a brass fence across the middle. On one side there is a flock of white sheep; on the other side, a flock of black sheep. Whenever the shepherd transfers a sheep from one side to the other, it changes colour – from white to black, or vice versa. This reflects the way in which everyday reality turns into the supernatural in the Otherworld. It is also similar to the Chinese concept of yin and yang (female/male duality).

On the Island of the Revolving Beast, the beast moves faster than thought, turning endlessly around on itself and constantly changing from one species to another – a notion that recalls the shapeshifting powers of magicians, such as Taliesin (see pp.102–103) and of shamans in many cultures. The Celts understood that motion is the ultimate reality: flux gives life its meaning. In the words of a Greek philosopher, "No one bathes in the same river twice."

who murdered his father. Blown off course by a gale, the voyagers find themselves among the islands of the Otherworld. Rowing from land to land, they gradually learn the arts of temperance, humility and forgiveness (losing all three of Mael Duin's brothers in the process). After many years at sea, the surviving travellers decide to return home, and on the voyage back to Ireland they happen upon the island where the murderers live. No longer bent on revenge, Mael Duin displays his newfound magnanimity and extends friendship to the malefactors, even feasting with them and recounting his traveller's tales.

Like other *imrama*, this epic narrative is, to use modern terminology, an allegory about personal growth – for the reader as well as for the wanderers. Faced with countless choices, the travellers make moral decisions at every turn. If their

AN INVITATION TO PARADISE
. . . .

In the 14th-century tale *The Wooing of Etain* (poet unknown), the fairy
lord Midir invites his love to a utopian island in the Otherworld.

"Hair is like the blooming primrose there;
smooth bodies are the colour of snow.
In this place, there is neither mine nor yours;
bright are teeth, dark are brows ... .
Intoxicating the ale of Inis Fáil;
more intoxicating by far that of Tír Már ... .
Warm sweet streams throughout the land,
your choice of mead and wine.
A distinguished people, without blemish,
conceived without sin or crime."

choice violates any of the strict (yet hidden) rules, disaster ensues, including the loss of fellow travellers. Thus, crew members who stray onto the Island of Laughing or the Island of Weeping are forced to stay there for ever, becoming as obsessive as the other inhabitants – a warning against both excessive lightheartedness and self-indulgent grief. Voyagers who have committed some secret crime are carried off by giant birds – in the moral maze it is impossible to escape the consequences of one's actions. Those who attempt to steal treasure from Otherworld islands are themselves stolen away by monster cats – cosmic (even karmic) irony fits the punishment to the crime. However, those who successfully negotiate the pitfalls are permitted to reach the most complex and beautiful of the Otherworld islands, the Isles of the Blessed, or the Island of Women, where time stands still in an eternal spring and the inhabitants are immortal.

To set sail on an unknown ocean is to cast oneself into the hands of fate. Yet fate can never be merely neutral – there is always a moral dimension. Life itself is a quest, and the committed and conscientious seeker after truth and goodness will be appropriately rewarded in time.

During their long voyage on the "streams of the ocean", St Brendan – a 6th-century abbot and the hero of legendary travels – and his companions see a crystal column, covered with a silver net, floating in the sea. The column and net may have been the vivid description, characteristic of travellers' tales, of a sea mist that had collected around an iceberg. But in the story the crystal column contains a silver chalice with which St Brendan and his companions celebrate Mass.

VISIONS OF
OUR ANCESTORS

Respect for the past and for ancestors is a common theme in Celtic wisdom. When St Patrick wished to record the tales of the ancient Celts for posterity, two pre-Christian Irish heroes, Oisin and Cailte, came back to the world of the living to retell their stories. In the following extract, from a 12th-century manuscript by an unknown poet, the heroes reminisce about the sacred Isle of Arran.

"Arran of the many stags, the ocean reaches up to its shoulder;
island where hosts are feasted,
a ridge where the dark blue spears are reddened.

Skittish deer on its mountain peaks, tender blue berries on its moors,
cold water in its streams, acorns on its brown oaks.

There are hunting hounds there, blackberries and sloes of the blackthorn;
dense thorn-bushes in its forests, stags wander in its oak-woods.

Lichen is gathered in its rocks, there is flawless grass on its slopes,
a sheltering cloak over its crags, gambolling deer-calves, leaping trout.

Its lowland is smooth, its swine are fat, its fields are pleasant,
as you can believe;
There are nuts on the hazel-boughs, longships sail past it.

When fair weather comes it is delightful;
There are trout under its riverbanks;
Seagulls call to each other around its white cliff;
Arran at all times is delightful."

The following extract is taken from the medieval Irish poem, *The Colloquy of the Two Sages*. The chief poet Ferchertne challenges a young man called Nede, who claims precedence over him as poet. The two debate, and Nede eventually wins, as his wisdom is from his forebears, who were gods, poets and magicians. In this passage, the two poets are discussing their contrasting prophecies.

"And you, young master, whose son are you?

Not hard to say, I am the son of Poetry,
Poetry is the son of Rhetoric ...
And Wisdom comes from the three sons of the
Goddess Brighid, daughter of the Dagda mor. ...
And you, my elder, who are your forebears?

Not hard to say. I am the son of Adam
Who was created without being born.
First buried in the womb of Mother Earth ...
A question, young master, what is your news?

Good news indeed is there:
A teeming sea, with the strand overrun with ships.
The woods smile into blossom, and the scythes do not cut them.
Trees bring forth fruit, corn grows in the fields.
Bees swarm throughout the radiant world ...
Everyone practises his own art.

Men perform valorous deeds …
A good man is the source of good advice.
These are my teachings.
And you, my senior, what are your tidings?

Terrible is my news, of the end of the world when
There will be many lords and few honours, when the living
Will give false judgment.
Cattle will be barren …
Evil men and usurpers will outnumber lawful kings.
Art will be debased and falsehood will prevail. …
Trees will lose their fruit as a witness to false judgments.
The man who follows a winter path will perish
Wolves will harry him through darkness and desperation and despair …
Thereafter will come plagues: sudden awful tempests
Will make the trees cry with the strike of thunderbolts. …
It will be the Last Judgment my son,
Great news, awful news, a time of terror.
Do you know, O young in age and great in knowledge, who is above thee?

Easy to say.
I know my God creates the wisest of prophets.
I know the hazel of poetry.
I know the mighty God.

THE WISDOM OF WATER

Water, over or under which so many mysterious realms exist, is an apt symbol of the truth beneath the surface of things – a kind of translucent veil between this world and the worlds beyond, in some ways clear, in other ways opaque. Through the magic power of water we are able to experience the wisdom of the Otherworld. This can be a matter of profound reflections on life, but also of simple revelations: the poet Neidne mac Adhna (see pp.74–5), walking along the seashore one day, heard the sound of wailing, and when he stopped to listen the waves revealed to him the imminent death of his father.

Oceans, rivers, streams and lakes all disclose the wisdom of water, but the well or spring has a special place in Celtic lore. Water that emerges from the ground as if by magic is imbued with revelatory powers of special intensity. In one story the Irish hero Cormac is lost in a mist and, when it clears, he finds himself beside a well. He soon learns that five salmon live in the well, eating the hazel nuts that fall from nine hazel trees growing near by. Also, five rivers flow from this source. Cormac realizes that this is the Well of Knowledge (see p.79): the rivers flow into the five provinces of Ireland, and represent the five senses, from which all human knowledge derives.

This wooden pilgrim statuette, dating from the 1st century CE, is a votive offering. It was found at a site at the source of the River Seine in France. An offering brought prosperity to the giver by encouraging the benevolence of the gods who resided in the water. The Greek historian Strabo tells of hoards of precious objects that were deposited in lakes.

In another tale a spring has the power to restore life to the dead, so long as the deceased has received love, honour and truth from his or her loved ones. When Finn mac Cumhaill's magical servant, the Gilla na Grakin, is killed, the Gilla's wife sails the ocean with his body, searching far and wide for a way to bring her husband to life again. Eventually, she lands on an island where she witnesses a dead bird regain its strength and fly away. The wife's devotion is rewarded. On this island she finds a magic spring; and when she places a few drops of springwater on her husband's lips, sure enough, he comes to life in front of her eyes.

COVENTINA'S WELL

· · · · · · · · · · · ·

At Carrawburgh on Hadrian's Wall lie the ruins of a Romano-Celtic site dedicated to Coventina, the goddess of the spring that feeds the well here. Nymph-like, she is shown on a carving pouring water from a pitcher. Just as, today, we might throw coins into a well, devotees left votive offerings for Coventina, including pins and carvings. Among the objects found was a human skull, left perhaps to help its owner's spirit pass safely into the afterlife.

VESSELS OF TRUTH

Because water, the essence of life, is also a potent source of wisdom and truth, accessible to poets, druids, kings and heroes, the cauldron and the cup, being containers of this magic fluid, carry a spiritual potency of their own. This symbolism is complemented in the legend of the Holy Grail, by an association with blood. Sometimes the grail is a vessel that contains a bloody head, an early Celtic symbol, or in the more Christian version it is a chalice used to catch the blood of the dying Christ. The cauldron is also linked with rebirth and with inexhaustible plenty: the Irish god the Dagda possesses, in addition to his club of destruction, a vessel from which he dispenses a never-ending supply of food.

During the Middle Ages a Welsh monk composed a poem about a raid into the Otherworld, in which he took on the voice of one of the most famed prophets – Taliesin, chief of bards. The author, merging the pagan and Christian symbolism of the chalice, describes how Taliesin sails with King Arthur and the ancient heroes of Wales in the ship *Pridwen* to capture a magic Otherworld cauldron, decorated with jewels and pearls. They enter a strange, almost surreal, world in which images

There is an obvious practical association between large communal vessels and hunting – the cooking pot, like the spring, was a source of life itself. In this ceremonial object from southern Austria, dating from c.650BCE, a cauldron, which perhaps served a practical purpose as an incense burner, dominates a group of stags and hunters. The piece is set on wheels, possibly for use in a hunting ritual.

of glass towers and fortresses appear fleetingly on Otherworld islands. The cauldron is eventually captured but the cost is high – only seven of the company who set out on the voyage return to their homeland.

Another tale, which shows how the High King Cormac gains wisdom from a boiling vessel and earns himself two precious gifts from the Otherworld, exemplifies the way in which a cauldron may serve as a profound image of truth.

One May morning a splendid warrior approaches the walls of Tara, carrying a silver branch bearing three golden apples from which issues sweet music with the power to comfort people and lull them into a healing sleep. The visitor reveals that he has come from a land of truth, where there is no sickness or decay, and no sadness, envy or hatred. As a token of his friendship, he offers the High King Cormac the silver branch in return for three favours.

The king accepts this proposition, and a year later the warrior returns to redeem his promise. First, he asks for Cormac's daughter; then his son. Cormac grants these favours and uses the powers of the silver branch to allay the sadness of the court at the loss of the royal children. When the warrior next demands Cormac's wife, the king reluctantly consents, but then sets off with his men in pursuit of the visitor. Suddenly, a mist descends on the company, and Cormac finds himself alone beside a walled fortress, which is also the place of the Well of Knowledge. A handsome stranger and his beautiful female companion offer Cormac the hospitality of the fortress. Soon a man enters carrying a pig. He cuts the animal into four quarters and tosses the meat into a "cauldron of truth". The man tells Cormac that the meat will cook only if a true tale is told for each portion. The pig-owner, the host and his companion each tell a true story, and their portions are duly cooked. Then Cormac tells the tale of the disappearance of his family, and his pork is also cooked. However, Cormac, a man of great honour and integrity, refuses to eat without his warband. The host sings the king to sleep, and when Cormac wakes up he is surrounded by his family and his men.

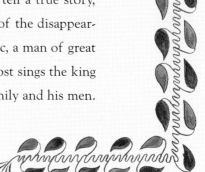

THE VOYAGE OF TADG

• • • • • • • • • • •

The tale of Tadg mac Cein, first told in Ireland in the 14th century, shows how a vessel from the Otherworld (given in recognition of Tadg's honesty) can lend authority to the hero's position as ruler of his kingdom.

When raiders kidnap his wife and brothers, Tadg sets sail with a band of warriors to rescue them. The first island they come to is full of beautiful birds. However, the men eat the birds' eggs and this violation causes them to sprout feathers – hardly fitting attire for warriors on a rescue mission. Fortunately the feathers soon drop off. The next island reached by Tadg and his men is inhabited by all the Irish people who have lived before them – it is the Otherworld. Here, the hero is given a goblet and three musical birds (to guide his onward journey) by an Otherworld woman. The vessel is significant in two ways. It was found in the heart of a whale, a creature that has magic powers, and it is given to Tadg by an Otherworld woman – often a symbol of sovereignty in Celtic tradition.

Confident of his worthiness as a leader and guided by the birds, Tadg sails on to fight a fierce battle against the raiders and rescue his wife and brothers.

Later that same night the king admires the workmanship of his host's golden cup. The host tells Cormac that the cup will break when three lies are told but become whole again after three truths are uttered. He then tells three lies, so that the beautiful object shatters. Then he assures Cormac that while his wife and daughter were away, no man touched them, nor did his son sleep with a woman. To Cormac's amazement the cup becomes whole again. The host finally reveals himself to be Manannan mac Lir (see p.52), the mysterious visitor who had given Cormac the silver branch. In an instant Cormac finds himself back on the Plain of Tara with his wife, family and warband, holding the "cup of truth" in his hand. Thus, a great king is made greater because he is deserving of two precious gifts from the Otherworld – the silver "branch of comfort" and the "cup of truth".

IN THE GUISE OF A SWAN

The grace and beauty of the swan, with its elegant, long neck and soft, white feathers, make it a natural symbol for all that is good, sacred and pure. Able to glide on a river or lake, waddle on land or beat powerfully through the air, the swan also links the watery Otherworld with the realms of earth and sky. The swans of the Otherworld are shapeshifters, able to change form at will, and are identifiable by the gold or silver chains that hang around their necks (see opposite).

Like so many inhabitants of the Otherworld, the swan is an ambiguous creature, with a dark aspect that counterbalances its positive qualities. In the story of the children of Lir – a tale so sad that it qualifies as one of the "Three Sorrows of Storytelling" – the widowed King Lir remarries so that his daughter Fionuala and his three sons might have a new mother. But the new queen is jealous of the king's affection for his children, and so she uses sorcery to transform them into swans. However, the swan-children are able to retain their powers of speech and their musical abilities, and people come from far and wide to listen to them sing on the lake and to take comfort from their music.

After many sad adventures, the unhappy swan-children meet a hermit who is able to offer them consolation for their plight through the Christian faith. But their suffering is not yet completely over, as a wicked king captures and steals the swans, whereupon their plumage falls out to reveal four ancient, shrivelled creatures. Realizing that they will now die, the swan-children ask only to be buried together in one grave, and the kindly hermit grants their request. Thus the children of Lir find peace at last and are able to enter the kingdom of heaven.

In the Arthurian tale of Lohengrin, son of Sir Percival, the boy first appears in this world in a boat that has travelled from the Otherworld, drawn by a beautiful white swan. Lohengrin is often depicted wearing white (recalling the feathers of the swan) in recognition of his supernatural beginnings.

THE DREAM OF OENGHUS MAC OG

· · · · · · · · · · · ·

Oenghuș is the son of the Dagda and the goddess Boinn. For a whole year he pines for a beautiful woman who comes to him every night in a dream. His parents are unable to help him find her, so they consult King Bodb, who is famed for his occult knowledge. Bodb takes Oenghus to a lake on which there are a hundred and fifty swans, all wearing neckchains, and tells him that the swans are able to spend every other year as women. The change takes place at Samhain, a time of transformation. Oenghus is told that if he can correctly identify his dream-love among the swans she will become his for ever. At the following Samhain, Oenghus returns to the lake to find his love. He chooses the only swan wearing a gold chain, rather than a silver one. This swan is Ibormeith, his dream-love. Overjoyed to have found each other, the swan and the man embrace. Then both fly away together as swans, linked eternally by the gold chain.

FATE AND
FOREKNOWLEDGE

How can we know what fate has in store for us? Only by consulting druids, prophets or poets. Druids impressed Roman visitors with their ability to unlock the patterns of the future by observing the flight of birds, the phases of the moon or the movement of the stars. Women were also seers, often predicting the outcome of battles and the fate of heroes. And every Celtic king had his own poet skilled in the writing of prophetic verse.

OUR YESTERDAYS ARE OUR TOMORROWS

Those who wish to predict the future must first be acquainted with the past – which is why Celtic seers and magicians begin their prophecies by looking back in time, not forward. Their experience and learning gives them an "accurate knowledge of the goodly race", which they use as the basis for their predictions.

These gifted souls list their experiences in a litany of past lives, which lends authority to their powers. Often they have shapeshifted to become animals, plants or aspects of nature, such as the wind or the rain; and in this form they have witnessed historic events. The more diverse their guises, the more knowledge they can gather to pass on to others. Amergin, the seer of the Tuatha De Danann, remembers his experiences as a salmon, a bull and a boar, as well as the time that he spent as the wind and as a wave. Tuan MacCairhill, one of the first invaders of Ireland, was by turns a deer, a boar and finally an eagle.

Sometimes periods lived as an animal or a natural phenomenon are interspersed with experience as an inanimate object. After the boy Gwion had taken the form of a grain of wheat, he was swallowed by the witch Ceridwen, who had turned herself into a hen. He was then reborn as the bard Taliesin (see pp.102–103). A catalogue of the poet's past lives is written in the *Book of Taliesin*: "The second time I was created, / I was a blue salmon. / I was a dog, I was a stag; / I was a roe-buck on the mountain side, / I was a treasure chest, I was a spade; / I was a hand-held drinking horn; / I was a pair of fire-tongs for a year and a day; / I was a speckled white cock among the hens of Eiden, I was a stallion standing at stud; / I was a fierce bull; / I was

grain growing on the hillside. / … . The hen, my enemy, red-clawed and crested, swallowed me. / For nine nights I was a little creature in her womb; / I was ripened there. / I was beer before I was a prince. / I was dead, I was alive."

The older prophets tend to have lived close to nature for a long time. For example, the great magician Merlin of Arthurian legend spends many years among the apple trees, conversing with a little woodland pig. The notion that animals can themselves see the future follows on from a belief in the wisdom of nature. Famous prophecies are attributed to the salmon and the trout. Species that live in the shadowy world under water quietly mature into venerable sages, observing the world change around them as their ever-increasing knowledge makes their foresight grow stronger. As with humans, the experiences gained during a long life provide a guarantee of the creatures' wisdom. The Celtic respect for

The Welsh rallied to Henry Tudor under the banner of the red dragon, an ancient symbol of Welsh rule. But after the Battle of Bosworth in 1485 the Tudor rose began to replace the older motif. Prophets still had credibility in the fifteenth century despite laws passed against their practices. When a spy reported that the Welsh still believed in the prophecies of old, a clever poet, calling himself "Ambrosio Talgesino" (the Latin names for Merlin and Taliesin) subverted these laws. He claimed Taliesin's prophecy that Welsh kings would again reign in Britain had come true with Tudor rule: "since everything which has been said here has come to pass, it is possible to read and write this without scandal. And if there is an error, let it be forgiven the old poet."

THOMAS THE RHYMER

· · · · · · · · · · · ·

One of the most famous Scottish prophets is Thomas of Erceldoune, known as Thomas the Rhymer, who lived in the 13th century. According to one tradition, he visits the Otherworld in the company of an amorous fairy queen who rewards his devotion by giving him the precious gift of prophecy. However, in the following alternative version of the tale, Thomas's power comes to him by birthright rather than through service.

Thomas's mother dies before her son is born. The grieving husband visits his wife's grave one night and finds there a baby boy, who is half in and half out of the earth. He names this child Thomas and raises him as his own. When Thomas grows up, he returns to his mother's grave. There he finds a book of prophecy, mysteriously placed, just as he had been as a baby, half in the world of the living and half in the world of the dead.

longevity is conveyed well in the story "Oldest Animals", which tells of the search for Mabon, son of Modron. Culhwch, Cei and Bedwyr set out with Gwrhyr, who knows the language of birds and beasts, to find where Mabon is held prisoner. Gwrhyr first approaches the Ouzel of Cilgwri. "Look at that anvil," the bird tells him. "Ever since I was a young bird I have cleaned my beak on it each evening. It is now the size of a nut. No, I do not know where your prisoner is, but maybe my old friend the Stag of Rhedynfre can help you."

They approach the stag and ask him the same question. The stag shakes his magnificent antlers. "When I first came here, that oak stump was a sapling. It grew into a tree but now it is no more than a stump. I do not know where your prisoner is, but I will take you to the animal that God made before me." They find the Owl of Cwm Cawlwyd, but he, too, is unable to help: "My wings have worn to mere stumps and this valley has been laid waste many times. But I will take you to the oldest creature in the world and perhaps he will know." The owl leads them to where the Eagle of Gwenabwy perches on a small, weathered stone. When the owl asks him if he knows where Mabon is, the old eagle says, "This stone was once a great rock; now it is worn away. But I know nothing of the man you seek. Once when I was hunting in Llyn Llyw, I sank my claws into a great salmon who drew me down into the lake. We were enemies until one day he came to me to have fifty fish-hooks removed from his back. If he doesn't know, no one will."

The eagle leads the men to the Salmon of Llyn Llyw, who puts his great head above the water and says, "Where the river washes the wall of Caer Loyw I can hear the moans of a prisoner in great distress. Get on my back and I will take you there." The men ride on the salmon until they reach the wall of Caer Loyw, a formidable prison. Outside, Cei calls out, "Who is lamenting?" "I am Mabon, son of Modron," comes the reply. The warriors then set him free and the salmon takes them all back where they came from. In this way, through the bravery of the warriors and the knowledge of the oldest creatures, Mabon was rescued.

THE WISDOM OF THE SALMON

Salmon, battling their way upstream in the river of their birth to their spawning grounds and leaping high against rushing waterfalls, resist the flow of tide and time, and hence are special creatures. Mysterious, valiant and resolute, they are fitting messengers between worlds, and by extension they are the embodiment of knowledge. Old salmon, their backs riddled with the hookmarks of unsuccessful fishermen, speak and give advice to Welsh and Irish heroes. Eating the flesh of salmon confers the gift of prophecy on the deserving. Salmon swim in the rivers and wells of the Otherworld, feeding on the hazel nuts that fall from the "trees of knowledge", and sometimes passing into the human world to deliver prophecies of their own on "the manner of the world to come".

The way in which the salmon links our everyday reality with the Otherworld is illustrated in the story of a miracle performed by St Asaph. His sister was the

wife of Maelgwn Gwynedd, a powerful Welsh king, whose bad temper was legendary. One day the queen lost her wedding ring and her angry husband immediately jumped to the wrong conclusion and accused her of infidelity. Distraught, the queen appealed to her brother, St Asaph, for help. The saint directed Maelgwn to cut open a salmon that had been freshly caught that morning and, sure enough, the king found his wife's gleaming wedding band inside its stomach. The king then humbly acknowledged the power of the saint, and his wife's fidelity.

The best-known "salmon of knowledge" tale concerns the bard Finn Ecs, who seeks the fish's power, and Finn mac Cumhaill, the Irish hero (see below).

FINN MAC CUMHAILL

As a boy Finn mac Cumhaill is asked by Finn Ecs to watch over a fish cooking on a fire. It is a special "salmon of knowledge" and Finn Ecs plans to gain its power by eating it. But the boy's attention wanders and the fish burns. He touches it and scorches his thumb, which he then puts in his mouth, thus gaining the power of prophecy. When Finn Ecs returns, he realizes that the boy is the destined one, and becomes his teacher. Whenever Finn, as an adult, puts the burned thumb in his mouth, he sees into the future.

THE MYSTERY
OF THE HEAD

For the Celts, the essence of being, both physical and spiritual, resides in the head. The image of the head appears everywhere – carved in the round, or as a decoration on pillars, coins, cauldrons and altars. Charged with protective power, the head acts as a talisman to ward off evil. It is also a symbol of the divine and a reminder that life continues after death. Classical authors claim that the Celts took the heads of their enemies as battle trophies and hung them in temples or used the skulls as drinking cups, but Celtic narratives about heads present a more sympathetic picture of their tradition.

The story of Donn Bo, a young warrior famous throughout Ireland for his beautiful voice, focuses on the power of the head as a repository of continuing life long after the death of the body. Donn Bo promises his lord, Fergal, that he will sing for him at the victory feast after the forthcoming battle, but unfortunately both lord and singer perish in the fighting and their decapitated bodies are left on the battlefield. The night after the battle, one of the victorious soldiers wanders

Many Celtic stories tell of severed heads that offer protection. In one tale the head of Bendigeidfran mab Llyr accompanies his companions on their travels, enabling the men safely to attend Otherworld feasts that last for many years. When the carousing is over the men bury the head as Bendigeidfran requested. It then becomes a powerful talisman against sickness, and no plague can strike while it remains interred.

among the bodies, looking for a head to take back to his lord's hall where their victory feast will take place. Suddenly, through the darkness, he hears the melodic strains of a voice and comes upon the decapitated head of Donn Bo, singing to his dead master. The soldier picks up the head, takes it back to the hall and places it on a pillar in the midst of the feast. Upon hearing how the soldier found the head, the victorious lord addresses it courteously, requesting it to sing for him as it sang for Fergal. The head then turns away from the living and, staring into the darkness, sings a song so sweet and sad that everyone at the feast weeps.

THE COMPASSION OF ST MELLOR

St Mellor is a healing saint popular in Brittany and Cornwall, and the patron of several wells. After he was martyred, his head was stuck on his own crozier to be shown to the king. On the way the murderer carrying the crozier became tired and thirsty, and the gentle, forgiving saint took pity on him. He told the man to drive the crozier into the earth – whereupon it took root and became a tree in the shade of which the murderer could rest. Then a clear, healing spring bubbled up from the same spot to provide a drink for him.

BIRDS OF DESTRUCTION

War goddesses in the form of birds scream over battlefields and settle on the shoulders of those about to die. After the battle, crows, ravens and eagles feed on the dead. In this extract from the *Canu Heledd* cycle, Princess Heledd addresses the eagles that feast on the corpses of her brother King Cynddylan and his warriors, who died defending the town of Trenn on the Welsh border.

"Grey-crested eagle of Pengwern, tonight
from on high it shrieks,
greedy for the flesh of the one I love.

Grey-crested eagle of Pengwern, tonight
from the heights it cries,
greedy for Cynddylan's flesh.

Grey-crested eagle of Pengwern, tonight
is its talon opened wide,
greedy for the flesh I love.

Eagle of Pengwern, from afar it calls tonight,
searching for the blood of men.
Trenn will be called an unfortunate town.

Eagle of Pengwern, from afar it calls tonight,
searching for the blood of men.
Trenn will be called a blood-specked town."

GUARDIANS OF THE SOUL

A society that gives credence to an unworldly dimension of life – the profound truths that lie beyond the veil of the usual – is one that will invest its faith in talented specialists who are able to mediate between the two worlds: the seer, the druid and the bard. With the coming of Christianity, saints joined the roster of gifted guardians of the soul – and many previously pagan figures acquired a new name and a fresh set of saintly qualities.

THE WISDOM
OF THE DRUIDS

Druids, together with bards and seers, are the custodians of wisdom in the Celtic world. The classical author Diodorus Siculus gives a detailed account of how they acquire their knowledge. He explains that the title "druid" means "one who is very knowledgeable", and that the understanding which the druids possess is either *fis*, "secret knowledge", or even *im fiss*, "complete secret knowledge".

In order to use this knowledge, Diodorus Siculus explains, a druid performs a special ritual called *imbas forosnai*, or "knowledge of enlightening". He takes a small piece of flesh from a sacred animal, such as a pig or a horse, which has been cooked specially for the ceremony. Having chewed this piece of flesh, he places it on the flagstone behind the door of his house. Then he sings an incantation over the morsel and offers it to the gods. The knowledge he seeks visits him in a dream of revelation. If the dream does not come immediately, however, he chants again, this time reciting the incantation into the palms of his hands. After that he sleeps

The druids practised divination (that is, the art of predicting the future) by augury and by animal sacrifice. They looked at birds in flight and made prophecies based on the patterns they made. They were also able to foresee future events by cracking open the bones of certain animals, including dogs and cats, and chewing the marrow. Also, if they drummed their fingers while chanting, and then touched someone, they could tell that person's fate.

with his hands pressed to his cheeks to intensify the power of his magic words. His colleagues keep watch so that no one disturbs him in this trance-like state. When he awakes, he finds himself in possession of the understanding he sought.

Divitiacus is one of the few druids to be mentioned by name in the classical sources. The leader of the Aedui, a Gaulish Celtic tribe, he was respected for his statecraft by Julius Caesar, who describes him as noble-minded. Divitiacus was a friend of the Roman philosopher Cicero, who tells us that the druid claims to be conversant with the Greek science of *physiologia* (the knowledge of nature), and that he could predict events by augury (see opposite).

PLINY ON DRUIDS

Pliny notes the importance of the oak tree to the Celts, and uses this as the basis for a fanciful explanation of the meaning of the word "druid": "The druids – for so their magicians are named – held the mistletoe sacred above all and the tree that supports it, always supposing that tree to be the oak. They choose groves formed of oaks for the sake of that tree alone. They never perform any of their rites except in the presence of a branch of oak; so that it seems probable that the priests themselves may derive their name from the Greek word for that tree. The druids think everything that grows on the oak has been sent from heaven, and that the tree was chosen by the god himself."

CATHBAD

· · · · · · · · · · · ·

Cathbad, the principal druid of King Conchobar of Ulster, is a wise and far-sighted adviser. He alone has the authority to speak before the king does. Cathbad embodies the human aspects of the druid's role as the teacher of the Ulster warrior's sons. He specializes in prophecy, and thus is able to predict the most auspicious days for the boys – including his most illustrious pupil Cuchulainn, the future hero – to take up arms. But despite his skill in foreseeing the future, Cathbad has no control over fate. He predicts at the time of Deirdre's birth (see p.16) that the beautiful child will bring ruin to the king, but Conchobar ignores this advice with disastrous consequences. He also tries unsuccessfully to help Cuchulainn to defeat a plot hatched by hostile magicians.

The privileged status of the druids can have disastrous consequences for anyone who shows them disrespect, whether intentionally or not, as demonstrated by Cathbad, chief druid of King Conchobar (see opposite). On the eve of a battle one of the king's champions shouts out a warning before Cathbad has a chance to speak. This transgression of the druid's right to precedence is so serious that the man's horse rears up beneath him and he loses control of his weapons, so that his shield flies out of his hand and decapitates him.

The Greek author Strabo reports: "The druids say that men's souls and the universe are indestructible, although both fire and water will at some time or other prevail over them." Druids have a special relationship with water: they can cause rivers and lakes to dry up and can summon storms against their enemies. But in an even greater example of their control over the elements, the druid Figol manages to meld fire and water: when the Tuatha De Danann prepare to fight the monstrous Fomorians, Figol promises that by his magic, fiery rain will fall on the enemy, not just once but three times.

In another tale, Dallan, a druid whose name means "the blind one", is asked to use his psychic abilities to find a missing woman. He makes four rods of yew and inscribes them with ogham letters – the mysterious writing druids use. His power intensified by these ritual objects, the blind druid uses the vision of his inner eye to "see" that the woman is being held captive inside a *sidh* mound.

While all chief druids predict events concerning their ruler and his kingdom, Beag mac De, druid at the court of High King Diarmid mac Cearrbheoil, has other, surprising abilities – he is able to foresee the future power of the Irish saints and has visions of St Brendan, St Ciaran and St Columba. Beag is rewarded before his death when he meets St Columba, who administers the Christian sacraments to the druid as a mark of special favour. Such affinity between pagan and Christian holy men symbolizes the way in which Christianity embraced aspects of ancient Celtic wisdom and assimilated them into its own traditions.

MAGICAL CONTESTS

The ability to change shape at will, to take on the guise of another person, an animal or even an object, is a special power, possessed only by the greatest of magicians. Shapeshifting skills are often tested to the full when two magicians pit their supernatural strength against each other, a theme common in Celtic stories. The most famous of these contests is that between the formidable witch Ceridwen and a young boy who acquires magical powers by accident.

Ceridwen has an ugly son, Avagddu, whose name means "darkness". She wishes to give him the gift of prophecy to compensate for his appearance. The witch mixes special herbs in a steaming cauldron and sets a little boy called Gwion Bach to watch the brew. When the mixture reaches boiling point, three drops of "liquid knowledge" splash from the cauldron and Gwion swallows them. Then the cauldron breaks and its contents run into the river, poisoning the king's horses when they drink from it. Gwion, realizing that he is now in mortal danger from Ceridwen, flees, with the witch in hot pursuit. He turns into a fish and dives

into the river, but she changes into an otter and pursues him. Next, Gwion becomes a hare, whereupon she turns into a greyhound to chase him. He then changes into a bird and tries to fly away, but she becomes a hawk and swoops after him. Finally, the young magician turns into a grain of wheat and Ceridwen changes into a black hen which swallows the grain. Nine months later the witch gives birth to a baby, one so beautiful that she cannot kill him (see pp.86–87). Instead, she puts him in a black bag, and drops it in the river, where it is later found by a prince who bemoans his bad luck at finding a baby and no fish. But then the child's true identity is revealed; for he is Taliesin, destined to become chief of bards (see p.11).

THE BRETON BOY AND THE MAGICIAN

· · · · · · · · · · ·

Even a mighty magician can be outwitted, as happens when a young Breton gets the better of Merlin. A princess falls in love with an apprentice magician and plans to marry him against the king's wishes. So the king deviously sends the young man to steal Merlin's ring and harp so that the irate Merlin will come to the court and stop the marriage. The lad searches for seven  days through seven woods until he finds a branch bearing thirty golden leaves. With this the boy lulls Merlin to sleep and then steals the ring and harp. When Merlin awakes he journeys to the court, not to prevent the marriage as the king had hoped, but to congratulate the young Breton magician on outsmarting him and to acknowledge the boy's magical prowess.

THE FORTRESS OF LOVE

His character based on the historical Roman emperor Maxentius, the Welsh hero Macsen Wledig has the gift of premonition. This story, from the medieval *Red Book of Hergest*, tells how, in a dream, Macsen foresees his journey to a great fortress where he meets the beautiful Elen of the Hosts – the woman who is later to become his wife after they meet in the exact circumstances foretold.

"In the dream which he [Macsen] saw, he was travelling along a river valley to its source and there he saw a high mountain, the tallest in the world. It seemed to him that the mountain reached up to heaven. And when he had crossed the mountain to the other side, he could see that he was walking in the loveliest, most level countryside that anyone had ever seen. Great rivers flowed from the mountain down toward the sea, and he walked along their banks to their estuaries.

After a long journey he came to the greatest port that anyone had ever seen. He saw a great city at the mouth of the river in which there was a great castle with many towers of different colours. He beheld a fleet of ships anchored at the river's mouth. And this fleet was the greatest fleet that man had ever seen, with one ship bigger and more beautiful than the rest. From what he could see of this ship, it had planks of gold and silver above the water-line. An ivory bridge led from the craft to the land and, in his dream, he could see himself crossing it onto the ship. A sail was raised and the ship set off over sea and ocean.

Eventually the ship came to the most beautiful island in the world. And when he explored from the sea on one side, across the island to the sea on the other side, he could see valleys, cliffs and high crags and a hard, rough land whose like he had never seen before. He espied another island out at sea, facing the hard, rough land. Between him and this island he saw a land whose plain was as broad as its sea and its mountain the length of its forest. A river flowed down from this mountain to the sea and at its mouth was a great fortress, the greatest that he had ever seen. The gate was open and so he entered.

Inside the fortress he beheld a fair hall. It seemed to him that the roof was made of gold, that the walls were of precious stones and that the doors were entirely of gold. In the hall he saw golden benches and silver tables. And on the bench across from him, he saw two auburn-haired young men playing *gwyddbwyll*. The game-board was of silver and thereon were golden pieces. The young men were dressed in rich black brocade. Their hair was adorned with circlets of red-gold inset with … gems and rubies and imperial stones. On their feet were new leather shoes, buckled with red gold. And at the base of

one of the pillars in the hall, he saw a snowy-haired old man sitting in a chair carved with two eagles of red gold. Golden armbands were on his arms and his hands were adorned with gold rings. A golden collar was around his neck and a gold band encircled his head. There was an air of authority about him. He had a golden *gwyddbwyll* board in front of him and in his hands he held a gold rod and a file. He was carving pieces for the game.

He [Macsen] saw a girl sitting near him in a red-gold chair. She was so beautiful that looking at the sun at its brightest would be no harder than looking at her. She was wearing a shift of white silk, the bodice fastened with clasps of red-gold. Over this she wore a brocade surcoat and a mantle which was fastened with a red-gold brooch. [She wore] a circlet, inset alternately with rubies ... and pearls and imperial stones, and a belt of red-gold. She was the loveliest girl that any man had ever seen. And the girl stood up from the golden chair and came toward him and he took her in his arms. And they sat down in the golden chair which was as comfortable for them both as it had been for the girl on her own."

THE WISDOM OF INSPIRATION

The word "inspiration" suggests breathing (inward *respiration*). For the Celts, such knowledge comes by air and water, and these two images are often combined. The Celtic version of these ideas is the "liquid breath of inspiration" or *awen*. Only after a perilous journey in which the soul travels outside the body, perhaps as far as the realm of the dead, can *awen* possess the spirit. As preparation for attaining this supernatural wisdom, the druid must sharpen his senses by going into a trance – an ancient technique used to reach the spirit world by shamans in many cultures around the world.

Gerald of Wales mentions "certain persons in Cambria [Wales], whom you will find nowhere else, called *awenyddion*, or 'people inspired' ". He goes on to describe how, when asked to predict the outcome of a forthcoming event, they roar violently, as if possessed by a spirit. They do not deliver the answer in a rational manner, but anyone who listens carefully can decipher the prophecy from among the apparently incoherent noises they utter. These shamanic druids do not return fully to their senses until they are shaken violently from their trance, as from a deep sleep; nor can they remember the replies they have given. Gerald also notes that the *awenyddion* receive spirit favours during their journeys. Some seem to have sweet milk or honey poured on their lips. Others claim on awaking that they have been given information in writing, as a spirit gift. The report of a cult statue depicting Ogmios, god of inspiration, provides support for Gerald's word-picture of shamanic trance. A chain links the ears of the devotees to the god's tongue, a graphic illustration of the extra-sensory nature of druidic inspiration.

Inspiration involves sight, hearing and speech. The Irish word for poet, *filidh*, derives from an ancient Indo-European root meaning "to see". Many Celtic triple-headed statues are linked where the ear should be, as if they share the sense of hearing (see p.111). However, the most important of the seer's faculties is the power of speech. The wisdom that the druid hears and sees on his journeys into the spirit realm is transmitted to his people through speech, and the *awenyddion* experience their gift as an opening of the mouth.

The importance of speech to the Celts comes through strongly in the following tale. Matholwch, an Irish king, violates the laws of hospitality by trying to kill his guest, Bendigeidfran mab Lyr. During the ensuing fighting many of Matholwch's soldiers are killed, and because their master has behaved so

THE DRUID'S EGG

· · · · · · · · · · ·

Pliny, in his *Natural History*, refers to the druid's egg, which he terms the *anguinum*. He describes a round, apple-sized talisman said to be formed from the spittle of angry snakes. Perhaps aptly, given the serpentine connection, druids used these eggs to give power to their tongue – to increase their chances of victory in the law courts through unassailable rhetoric. Groups of egg-shaped amulets that roughly resemble Pliny's description have been found at sites in Scotland, although no one has proved that they are actually druid's eggs.

THE BRAHAN SEER

· · · · · · · · · · ·

In the 17th century, Kenneth Mackenzie, the Brahan Seer, received his gift of prophecy from the dead. As a boy he usually accompanied his mother when she went to tend the family's cattle. One night, returning home late, they saw that the graveyard was full of spirits. Fearlessly, Mrs Mackenzie approached an open grave and placed her staff across it to prevent the spirit from returning. The ghost turned out to be a drowned princess who, in order to be allowed back into her grave, revealed the whereabouts of a strange blue stone that would bestow the gift of prophecy to her son, Kenneth. The young prophet's first experience of his new-found powers occurred soon afterwards when one night he dreamed of eating poisoned food. The following day when he was offered food by his jealous employer, he recalled the dream and refused it. Subsequently, Kenneth decided to venture out into the wider world where he felt that his gifts would be better appreciated.

dishonourably, they die under a cloud of shame. They are thus unable to make the transition into the Otherworld, so they are sent back from the land of the dead into the company of the living, deprived of the power of speech as punishment for their wrong-doing.

As if to set a proper value on the knowledge that can be gained from the spirit world, travels into that realm are extremely dangerous. The personal quest for supernatural wisdom has its dark side – out-of-body experiences can lead to death or dementia. Supernatural knowledge, if uncontrolled, can threaten even powerful seers with loss of reason. In one story, Merlin sees a vision so terrible that it drives him mad and he becomes a wild man, alienated from society. The ramblings of his troubled mind are heard only by his little pig companion and by the apple trees that provide shelter. When Gwenddydd, his sister, visits him in his woodland abode, she tries to give him comfort. First she offers him wine, but he rejects this. Then she offers milk, but this too he spurns. Only when she offers a third drink, of water, the purest liquid and the carrier of knowledge, does he accept. The water cures his madness and restores his abilities as a seer and prophet.

A ring of human heads encircles this pot, which was found at the site of Bavay in France. One of the heads is shown in triplicate, with three faces all rising from the same neck. They seem to be joined at the ears so that one face stares straight at the viewer and the two others are represented in profile. The number three has a great deal of significance in the Celtic wisdom tradition (see pp.114–115), and this triplicate face, which stands out among a band of other single faces, may also suggest heightened senses, such as those that a prophet or a bard might possess.

SAINTS AND ANGELS

In one of his most mystical poems, the bard Taliesin claims to come from the Land of the Seraphim. Such angelic beings are appropriate companions for the chief of bards, since seraphim are the highest of the orders of angels, the ones that hover closest to God's throne. The many angels depicted in the Book of Kells resemble those of Byzantium in form and dress, but when they communicate with Celtic saints these heavenly beings converse on matters relating to the Celtic wisdom tradition as well as Christian doctrine.

On one occasion St Patrick summons the ghosts of the old warriors Cailte and Oisin and their companions to tell him the adventures of the ancient Irish heroes and to recite to him the wisdom of the *ollamh*, the most important order of ancient Irish poets. Caught up in the midst of all this splendid pagan tradition, St Patrick begins to wonder whether he is neglecting his pastoral duties. Suddenly two angels appear to reassure him of the importance of the old heroes' tales, and St Patrick summons his scribes to take down the stories so that they can be preserved in written form for all time.

St Patrick's bell shrine is an elaborate bronze casket made in about 1100CE to house his bell, which continued to work miracles after the saint's death (see p.58). The silver-plating and filigree decoration contribute to its ornateness and reflect the exalted position held by St Patrick in Celtic Christianity. Written accounts of the saint's life refer to other miraculous possessions, such as that of a crozier. One account quotes a pagan prophecy: "The mitred-one will come, the end of his wooden staff bent," which foretells the coming of a saintly bishop carrying his staff of office.

The channel of communication between angels and Celtic saints is not just a conduit through which the word of God can spread to humankind – sometimes the angels require tasks to be carried out. This can be a perilous experience even for a saint, as the following tale about St Columba shows. One night while St Columba is meditating "in the rapture of his mind", he experiences an angelic vision. The angel asks him to preside over the investiture of an Irish king, and tries to hand him a glass book containing the words for the ceremony. When St Columba twice declines to take the book, the angel strikes him, marking the saint for life. The angel then asks him again if he will accept the book. This time the saint dares not refuse: he accepts the offering and proceeds with his commission.

THE HOLY BLACKSMITH

St Eloi is the Breton patron saint of blacksmiths. One day a stranger brought a horse that needed to be shod to Eloi's smithy. When Eloi agreed to help him, the stranger cut off the horse's legs, one by one, attached new shoes and restored the legs. The horse did not suffer during this curious incident. The stranger then revealed himself as Christ, who had come to honour the blacksmith. Eloi is also the patron of horses, and during his festival, or *pardon* – one of many that take place in Brittany – horses are ridden around churches so that the saint will protect them. Tufts of hair from the horses' manes and tails are offered to the saint.

THE POWER OF THREE

Triads (groups of three) and triplication run like a leitmotif throughout the Celtic world. Questions are asked three times, goddesses appear in threes and stone figures of the little hooded men who bring good luck always occur in groups of three. The number three has the ability to intensify power and to unify diverse experiences into a whole: sculpted heads and faces are carved in intertwined patterns so that the three become a single unit. These carved faces look to the past, the present and the future simultaneously, and any group of three images linked together in this way embodies the all-embracing nature of Celtic wisdom.

According to Julius Caesar, the druids refused to commit their knowledge to paper and instead passed on everything by word of mouth, entrusting it to memory rather than writing. They used a number of sophisticated mnemonic techniques, the most common of which is a triad of three elements. Groups of triads catalogue the laws, the rules of poetry and traditional knowledge of all kinds.

Such groupings make an invaluable mechanism for organizing and remembering the vast store of information for which a druid is responsible. Yet, as druids make little distinction between the sacred and the secular, the very act of putting knowledge into a triad elevates it to druidic lore. Often the real wisdom of the triad lies in a deeper meaning just below the surface, with the last element often carrying the most important message. The following triad records the three names of Britain: Merlin's Precinct, The Honey Isle and The Island of Britain. These epithets convey more than a simple historical record – they encapsulate the spiritual history of the island. It is a place of magic because of its association with the great magician Merlin; it is The Honey Isle because it is a fertile, prosperous land; but all these qualities and more, indeed its entire identity as a nation, are rolled up and concentrated into the last name of the three, which thus becomes charged with far more than literal significance.

TRIADS OF KNOWLEDGE

Triads of knowledge are an important vehicle for transmitting druidic and bardic wisdom. Some make wry observations on human frailty, while others emphasize serious truths about the human condition.

Three things it is best to do quickly:

Catch a flea as soon as you feel it;

Avoid the path of a mad dog;

Soothe contention.

The three fountains of knowledge:

Thought;

Intuition;

Learning.

The three functions of speech:

To recite;

To argue;

And to tell a story.

Three times for a fool's laughter:

At what is good;

At what is bad;

And at what he cannot understand.

Three kinds of men are there:

Men of God who return good for evil,

Men of this world who give good for good and evil for evil,

And the Devil's men who repay good with evil.

SPIRITUAL HEALING

The Roman writer Pliny describes a type of fern called *selago* that the Gaulish druids used for magical and medicinal cures. Since the plant has mystical as well as medicinal properties, it must be harvested according to the proper rituals. Before gathering *selago* offerings of bread and wine must be made, and whoever picks the fern must wear a white tunic and go barefoot. The plant may not be gathered with any iron implement, but must be picked by passing the right hand through the left sleeve of the tunic. If all these conditions are met, *selago* is a powerful charm against evil when worn as an amulet.

Caesar equates Celtic gods of healing with the classical sun god Apollo, but for the Celts the power to heal comes from the Otherworld, the realm of darkness and knowledge, not from the sun. Dian Cecht, the physician of the Tuatha De Danann who live in the Otherworld, is one of the most famous healers. After Dian Cecht's son Miach died, 365 healing plants grew from his grave. Each part of Miach's body produced a different medicinal herb. His father and sister gathered these herbs and placed them in the deep well of healing called Tiopra Slaine.

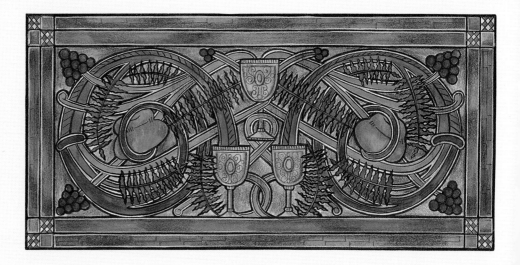

THE FAIRY FOUNTAIN

Healing is not just a matter of knowing the right cure; it also requires an appropriate attitude, as shown in a tale set in Finistère in Brittany. Two neighbours, Paol and Yon, set out for Paris. Paol, wealthy but with little regard for his fellow men, travels in comfort, while poor, honest Yon has to beg his way. One night Yon finds no shelter other than a hollow oak tree next to a strange fountain, which flows from east to west. At midnight Yon is awakened by a terrible noise – all around him *corrigans*, or fairy folk, are dancing. The leader, an ancient crippled *corrigan*, gloats that he has cast a spell on

the king's daughter, and only the water from this fountain can cure her. Unseen by the fairies, Yon manages to secure some magic water, and hurries to the palace where he cures the princess. Generous Yon tells Paol about the oak tree and fountain, and the schemer hurries off to find the magic place, with the intention of becoming a famous healer. He, too, hides in the tree and waits for the *corrigans*. But the fairy leader, enraged that a poor man has cured the princess, orders his companions to burn down the oak tree that harboured the thief, and greedy Paol perishes in the flames.

During the battle of Moytura, Dian Cecht and his remaining three children dropped the wounded warriors of the Tuatha De Danann into the well, chanting incantations over them; the warriors emerged with their wounds healed.

However, Dian Cecht's most amazing feat was to create a silver arm for Nuadu, king of the Tuatha De Danann. According to tradition, a maimed king cannot rule Ireland, and the loss of his arm excluded Nuadu from the kingship at a critical time for his people. In creating the silver arm, Dian Cecht performs an act of spiritual as well as physical healing, since he restores not just the king, but the institution of kingship itself.

The tale of the wasting sickness of Cuchulainn is a tale of illness and sadness brought on and cured by Otherworld knowledge. One day, at the feast of Samhain, Cuchulainn attempts to capture two mysterious swans that are linked together with a gold chain (see p.83). However, in order to escape the birds begin to sing a magic song so that Cuchulainn leans against a stone pillar and falls asleep.

A CHARM AGAINST SORROW

· · · · · · · · · · ·

The power of Celtic charms lies in the words themselves rather than their meaning. They must be spoken aloud. This charm is said when the night is black and the soul heavy with sorrow.

The charm of Michael with the shield,
Of the palm branch of Christ,
Of Brighid with her veil.
The charm that God set for himself
When the divinity within him was darkened.

In this enchanted sleep he has a dream vision in which two women come from the Otherworld and beat him until he falls senseless. When he wakes up, the hero takes to his bed and remains there for a year. As Samhain approaches again he returns to the stone pillar, and the two fairy women appear to him once more. This time they invite him to accompany them back to the Otherworld where, in return for defeating their king's enemies, he will have the love of the fairy woman Fand. The hero agrees and goes with them.

Cuchulainn fulfils his side of the bargain in the Otherworld and, enthralled by her, brings Fand back with him to live among humans. But his wife, Emer, berates Cuchulainn for his unfaithfulness, and the fairy woman is forced to leave him. The hero is inconsolable and wanders abroad like a madman. Emer asks the druids to help heal her husband, and they sing spells and incantations to quieten his wildness. Then they give him a drink of forgetfulness, and finally Cuchulainn is cured of his infatuation.

THE WISDOM
OF THE BARDS

The words of Amergin – "I am a word of skill" (meaning "I am a poet") – sum up the exalted position of poets and bards in the Celtic world. The bards are the keepers of tribal wisdom and by their craft they preserve the very identity of their people. The three privileges granted to all the bards of Britain are to have food and lodging everywhere in the land, to have weapons sheathed in their presence, and to have their word respected by all.

The value accorded a poet's words reflects the sacred nature of his learning, and the Irish laws set the honour-price of the chief poet, the *ollamh*, as equal to that of the king. One day while the druid Ollamhan, whose name means "chief poet", is sitting beside his brother, High King Fiachna, the sound of rushing wind is heard. The druid prophesies that his own son, who is soon to be born, will be Fiachna's equal. The jealous king summons his pregnant sister-in-law and questions her about the child, but she has no knowledge of the prophecy. However, as soon as he is born, the baby recites a poem. Fiachna, astounded at the child's

Feidhilm is the most famous female poet in Old Irish literature. Sometimes described as a sorceress, she is also a prophetess and forecasts doom for the forces of Queen Maeve of Connacht in her attempted invasion of Ulster. Feidhilm learned her craft in Scotland where the tradition of female poets was well established and several of them composed verse for Scottish clan chiefs.

precocious wisdom, accepts the boy as his equal and gives him Ollamhan's position as chief poet.

The sight, or *insight*, of Celtic poets works on three levels. It looks to the past wisdom of their world, it provides intuitive understanding of the present, and it allows them to foresee the future. Martin Martin, the 17th-century historian from the Isle of Skye, tells us that the Gaelic poets of his day learned their craft by lying in the dark with a stone on their chest. This druidic meditation helps to focus the mind and clear it of all distractions. With the help of this technique the bards of the period, like their Celtic forebears, were able to channel their consciousness in

REMEMBERING THE TAIN

• • • • • • • • • • •

One day, the bards of Ireland realized that they had forgotten the *Tain Bo Cuailgne*, the poem about the great cattle raid which pitted the men of Ulster against the men of Connacht. The saints of Ireland join with the poets to ask for God's help. So he revived one of the ancient heroes, who one last time recited the adventures of the men of Ulster, the fight between two magic bulls, the deeds of Cuchulainn and the wiles of Queen Maeve of Connacht. The scribes of Ireland then set down the poem so that future generations would have a sure means of keeping alive the deeds of the great heroes.

ways that enabled them to master the complexities of poetic composition, the intricate legal codes of the time, and the practical and occult knowledge which their calling required them to remember.

To be a bard is a vocation, a calling, and those who lack natural talent cannot make up for this with learning. There are many fanciful stories telling how bards acquired their gifts. The great dynasty of Irish bards, the O'Dalaighs, have a tale about their ancestor Cearbhall O'Dalaigh. As a boy Cearbhall worked for a farmer who asked the child every day whether he had seen anything unusual. The boy always replied in the negative, until one day he saw a cloud settle on a clump of rushes which were eaten by a brindled (streaked) cow. The farmer told Cearbhall to bring him the first milk from the cow, but Cearbhall spilled it on himself. Immediately the boy was transformed into a poet, speaking only in perfect verse. The farmer sent him away, and Cearbhall's fame as a bard spread as far as Scotland, where the king's daughter fell in love with him. Disapproving of his daughter's suitor, the king did everything in his power to keep the two apart. But Cearbhall lulled everyone except the princess to sleep with his sweet singing and harp-playing, and the lovers were finally able to come together.

While bards have the power to enchant with words, they are also able to inflict damage – some of the tongue-lashings they give can cause physical hurt. Even kings are subject to their wrath. According to the *Book of Invasions*, Cairbre, the chief bard of the Tuatha De Danann, composed the first satirical invective ever to be heard in Ireland, attacking King Bres with such scorn that the king's face broke out in blotches. As it was contrary to the laws of sovereignty for a blemished king to rule, King Bres was then deposed. This intemperance surfaces again in a 15th-century poem, in which Ireland's chief bard fights to hold back anger: "Before the wave of my fury surges up to burn the level cropland of your cheek, I will speak out against myself although I do myself an injury ... ." A bard's words of displeasure, though, are usually disgrace enough for their victims.

THE DUTIES OF A BARD

· · · · · · · · · · · ·

Celtic bards have great responsibilities. Young apprentices learn much of the knowledge that is required of them in the form of triads. The following examples enshrine some of the most important principles of bardcraft:

The Three Memory Feats of the Bards of Britain:

To know the history of the kings of Britain and Cambria;

To use language in all its glory;

To keep alive the genealogies and the descent of noble men.

The Three Foundations of Bardic Knowledge:

The knowledge of song;

The knowledge of bardic secrets;

The wisdom within.

The Three Pleasures of the Bards of Britain:

To speak knowledgeably;

To act wisely;

To bring peace and harmony.

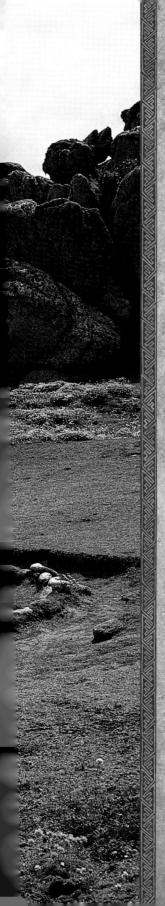

THE WISDOM OF ETERNITY

The Celts were fascinated by the image of the endless knot – a way to express infinity in a tangible pattern. The lines in knotwork on monuments and in manuscripts twist and turn, but always return to the starting point. In narratives of Otherworld journeys too, travellers have a wealth of experiences but eventually arrive back where they began. Viewed in this unworldly perspective, death is not an ending, but a doorway to eternal life.

THE CREATURES IN
THE PATTERN

The depiction of animals in Celtic art – on weapons, in stone carvings and, most spectacularly, in illuminated manuscripts – draws heavily on the wisdom of the Christian world as well as pagan traditions. Animals remind us of the vitality of nature, the divine gift of the world's variety and, through symbolic associations, the reality of the eternal.

Deservedly the best-known of Celtic illuminated manuscripts is the Book of Kells, a lavishly illustrated text of the gospels produced between the 7th and 9th centuries CE. Some of the animals featured most frequently in the manuscript are associated with Christ. The snake is a symbol of the Resurrection because it lives on, renewed, after shedding its skin, while the fish motif calls to mind the new converts to Christianity, swimming at their baptism (also, in Greek, the word for fish is an acronym for Jesus Christ, Son of God, Saviour). All the evangelists, except St Matthew who was personified by a man or an angel, were symbolized as animals: St Mark as a lion, St Luke as an ox and St John as an eagle. Birds portrayed in the Book of Kells include the peacock, which symbolizes Christ's incorruptibility, and the dove, which is linked with the Holy Spirit.

However, not all creatures in Celtic art have benign associations. In manuscript illustrations and in stone carvings there are many monsters, such as fire-breathing dragons, strange creatures who devour their own tails and reptile-like beasts depicted swallowing human victims (even, in one case, a bishop). Terrible though these creatures may be, they are tamed by the power of the Celtic saints. St Samson of Dol, revered in Cornwall and Brittany, was said to be able to turn a dragon to stone; and St Ronan rode a gigantic monster to an island to drive its poisonous inhabitants into the sea so that he could establish a monastery there.

THE PENITENTIAL MONSTER

· · · · · · · · · · ·

Among the most vivid images in Celtic illuminated manuscripts are those in which
a monster seems to be swallowing a human. These creatures, echoing the mysterious
man-eating monsters found on Celtic artefacts and in carvings, at the same time
conjure up the image of hell as a penitential beast that swallows sinners, such as
the one described in a medieval poem attributed to the poet Taliesin – a literary
mosaic that draws on poetic tradition, Christian legend and classical philosophy, all
animated by the sheer ebullience of the Celtic poet. This is the passage in question:

"I urged on rich fleets of ships.
I struck against a monster, finely scaled,
he had a hundred heads;
under his tongue a battalion of men,
another host of men in his throat;
like a toad with a forked black tongue,
one hundred nails in each claw;
like a speckled serpent with a crest,
one hundred sinful souls
are punished in his flesh."

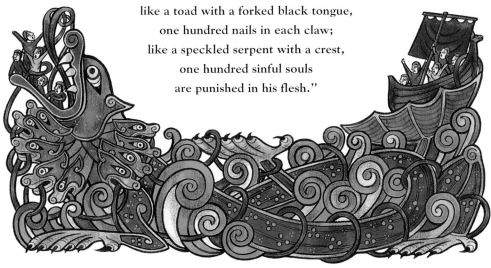

THE TWISTED VINE

Many of the patterns that are traced in manuscripts and carved on Celtic crosses depict vine-like plants growing in intricate, twisted shapes. Often these vines are rooted in a golden chalice, and among their intertwined leaves and branches grow bunches of grapes on which feed peacocks with iridescent, curling tail feathers. The Christian symbolism of the vine is a fusion of the Celtic and Byzantine wisdom traditions. The grape-laden vine that sprouts from a chalice represents Christ's promise of redemption; and the peacocks, depicted with their colourful tail feathers open, denote the Resurrection.

Even before this Christian symbolism became popular, plants played an important part in the Celtic imagination. One day three fairy women from Cruachan, a gateway linking the human world with the dark Otherworld, sit spinning yarn left-handed on twisted distaffs made of holly. To commit any act that goes against the movement of the sun – that is, with the left hand – is regarded as evil magic. The women's actions, combined with the magical properties of the twisted holly, enable the crones to ensnare two great heroes, Finn and Conan, in their yarn and bind them, with no way for them to escape. Finn's companions try to halt the malevolent spinning, but all except Goll mac Morna become entangled in the bewitched yarn. Goll finally slays the hags and rescues his companions.

The magical qualities of holly feature again in a tale of Taliesin. When Prince Elphin, the bard Taliesin's patron, boasts that his horses are better than those of King Maelgwn, the angry king insists on a horse race. Taliesin gives a stick made of holly to Elphin's jockey and instructs him to strike the hindquarters of each of Maelgwn's horses during the race. The jockey does so and the rival horses are no longer able to run. At the end of the race, Taliesin tells Elphin to dig at the place where the jockey throws down his hat and stick. Here, he discovers a cauldron full of gold. Thus, a delighted Elphin both wins the race and gains a hoard of treasure.

Many Celtic poems draw on the natural beauty and fragility of plants and use the imagery as metaphors for love. Thus the descriptive image of briar roses and holly growing from lovers' graves, twisting together for eternity, is often to be found in verse. Travellers to the Otherworld frequently return with tales of a land where it is everlasting summer and there are beautiful trees which produce fruit all year round. When humans eat the silver apples found growing on such trees, they long for Otherworld lovers.

HOLLY, IVY AND YEW

· · · · · · · · · ·

King Arthur tries to make peace between King Mark, the husband of Essyllt (Iseult or Isolda), and her lover Tristan. Arthur declares that one should live with her when the trees are bare and the other when they are in leaf. Her husband picks winter, when the trees are bare, as nights are longer then. Essyllt is jubilant – Mark's choice means that she will never be parted from Tristan, as she explains in the following extract from the 16th-century romance, *Tristan and Iseult*.

"Three trees there are and good ones too
The holly, ivy and the yew.
In leaf they are for every year.
Tristan's shall I be my whole life through."

THE ENDLESS KNOT

The Celts were drawn to interlaced patterns of great intricacy, reflecting a sheer joy in pattern and colour. Elaborate knots of lines and curves adorn weapons, mirrors, pottery and monuments. Similar patterns also appear in Celtic manuscripts, with clusters of curvilinear and geometric designs decorating individual letters, words, phrases and even entire pages. Here, we find human figures, birds and animals seemingly entangled in the interlacing line-work, their heads, hands and feet emerging with swirling flourishes. We see men grappling and pulling at each other's intertwined beards, and hounds chasing their prey through forests of abstract patterning.

Christianized Celts used interlaced designs in their manuscripts to reflect the eternal truths of the biblical message. The symbol of the endless knot, which expresses infinity through the pattern of a line that can always be traced back to its starting-point, is linked with the medieval legend of Solomon's seal, a magic ring decorated with mysterious symbols which enabled King Solomon to control the spirits. The shield that Gawain carries on his search for the Green Knight in the famous 14th-century poem is embellished with a five-pointed endless knot, which is described clearly, its connection with Solomon pointed out: "then they showed him the shield, that was a shining gules [red] / With a pentangle painted of pure golden hue … / It is a sign that Solomon set some while ago / As a token of fidelity, by virtue of its shape / For it is a figure that has five points / And each line overlaps and interlocks with another / And everywhere it is endless, and in England it is called / Everywhere, as I hear, the endless knot."

Many of the interlaced knots are formed from leaves and vegetation. The connection between the natural world and these stylized patterns is illustrated in the legend attached to the chapel at Locronan in Finistère, which is dedicated to St Ronan. After the saint's death several parishes quarrel over which should have

TURF LABYRINTHS

· · · · · · · · · · · ·

Shepherd boys in Cornwall and Wales played a game called Caer Droia. They cut the turf on the hillsides into a labyrinth, whose narrow pathway twisted and turned back on itself until it reached a central point. There were no false avenues or dead ends in these structures – the path always led to the centre.

The name Caer Droia may be derived from *caer y troiau*, Welsh for "the city of turnings". Perhaps the original purpose of such labyrinths was to provide a substitute for a journey of penance, or perhaps it was always simply a game that challenged the players to reach the heart of the maze in minimum time.

custody of his body and the honour of constructing his tomb. They place the saint's body on an ox cart and let the ox set off without a driver in the hope that the power of God will decide the site of the tomb by guiding the ox there. The parishioners follow behind. Toward nightfall the beast stops in a small wood on the top of a hill and the saint's followers go home. The next morning, when the people return, they are astonished to find that a chapel has been built already. The cart has miraculously turned into a stone tomb, and the branches of the trees in the wood have become petrified, forming the intricate stone tracery of the chapel that enshrines the saint's body.

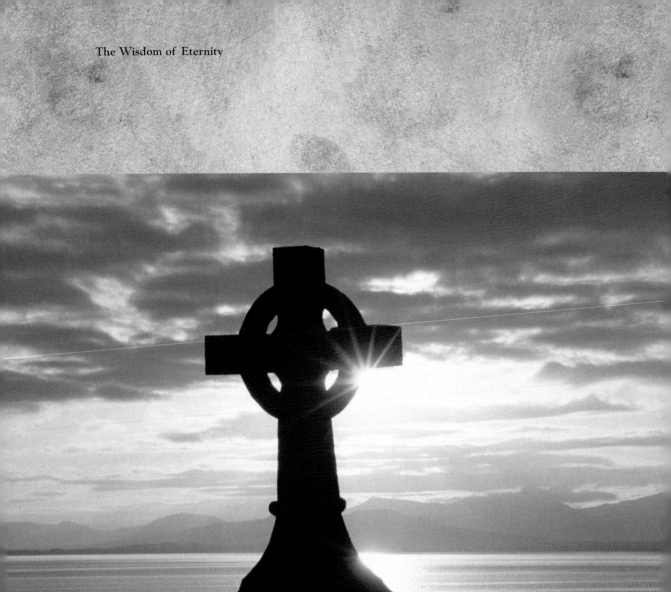

THE GREAT BARD

Celtic poetry and narrative contain numerous references to the cycle of living, dying and the afterlife. Celtic artists and writers use this vision in their representation of the cosmos as an eternal knot of experience, symbolized by the never-ending interlaced patterns that appear so abundantly in Irish manuscripts. In the following extract from the anonymous 13th-century *Book of Taliesin*, the chief bard in the title addresses us from Caer Siddi in the Otherworld. This passage features the characters Manawydan who is stepfather to Pryderi, the son of Pwyll, lord of Dyfed, and Rhiannon. When Pryderi is trapped in the Otherworld, Manawydan rescues him.

"A chair is prepared for me in Caer Siddi.
Old age afflicts none who is there –
this Manawydan and Pryderi know.
Three hosts play music before it,
and about its peaks flow the ocean streams;
And a bountiful fountain above it
whose water is sweeter than white wine.
And I will praise the lord on high
before that hidden place, the grave, brings peace to you."

HOW TO LIVE, HOW TO DIE

According to Diogenes Laertius, the druids expect all Celtic men to fulfil a triad of conditions in order to live a good life: they must worship the gods, they must do no evil and they must behave in a manly way. As with so many Celtic triads, the most important precept – manly behaviour – is listed last. "A man's memory does not age," runs a Celtic proverb. To leave behind a good reputation after death, and to be remembered by the bards, who praise the living and commemorate the dead, is every Celtic man's aspiration.

The Roman poet Lucan summarizes the Celtic attitude to death when he states, "Death is the middle of a long life." Grave goods were buried with their owners to ease the spirit's passage through the realm of the dead to the Otherworld. As well as weapons, many personal objects such as cups, hunting horns and even their chariots accompanied warriors, while jewelry and pottery were the main possessions interred with women. Food and drink were provided to give the soul sustenance on its journey. In addition to practical goods, some graves contained the bones of animal companions, such as horses and dogs, and models of wheels, which symbolized the eternal cycle of life and death.

This famous statue, known as *The Dying Gaul,* is a marble copy of an earlier bronze figure from the 2nd century BCE. He represents all that Greek and Roman commentators respected in their Celtic adversaries – a bold, primitive warrior (with the characteristic moustache), fighting naked except for his torc, his sword and the war trumpet lying beside him. The sounding of trumpets was part of the fearsome "Celtic charge" – as much a ritual as a military tactic, it prepared and inspired warriors to fight bravely and to the death.

LAMENT FOR A PRINCE

. . . . '

Llewelyn was the last native Prince of Wales, and his death (c.1282) represents the end of an era in Celtic history. The following extract from the 13th-century poem *Lament for Llewelyn ap Gruffudd*, by Gruffudd ab yr Ynad Coch, captures all the sadness of a people mourning the loss of their leader.

"With Llewelyn's death my mind fails me.
My heart is cold, fear is in my breast;
desire shrivels like kindling.
See you not the rush of wind and rain?
See you not oak trees buffet each other?
See you not the sea scouring the shore?
See you not the truth it portends?
See you not the sun hurtling through the sky
and that the stars have fallen?
Do you not believe God, foolish mortals?
See you not that the whole world is ending?
O God, let the sea cover the land –
why are we left to linger?"

PRONUNCIATION GUIDE

· · · · · · · · · · ·

The following guide to the pronunciation of Irish and Welsh covers only those sounds that differ significantly from how they might be pronounced in English. A simple guide to the pronunciation of individual names is also included in the index, in square brackets.

Irish
Words are usually stressed on the first syllable.

c	as **k** in **king**, never as **s**
bh	as **v** in **vine**
ch	before or after **a, o** or **u**: as **ch** in Scottish **loch**; before or after **e** or **i**: as the "rough" **h** in **hue** (= **ch** in German **ich**)
ll	before or after **e** or **i**: as the **lli** in **million** (= Italian **gl**)
mh	as **v** in **vine**
dh	as **th** in **then**
gh	before or after **a, o** or **u**, it is a sound which does not exist in English (= **g** in Spanish **agua**); before or after **e** or **i**: as **y** in **yes**
s	before or after **a, o** or **u**: as **s** in **say** and **yes**, never as **s** in **wise** before or after **e** or **i**: as **sh** in **shin**
th	as **th** in **thin**
a	as **a** in **mass** or **aw** in **pawn**
ae, ao	as **ay** in **say** (= French **é**)
ai	as **ee** in **see**, or **a** in **sat**, or **a** in **father**, or **aw** in **pawn**, or **i** in **sit**
e, ea	as **e** in **set** or **ay** in **say** (= French **é**)

ei	as **ay** in **say** (= French **é**) or **e** in **set**
i	as **i** in **sit** or **ee** in **see**
ia, io	as **ea** in **idea**
oe	as **oy** in **toy**
oi	as **o** in **top** or **aw** in **pawn**
ui	as **oo** in **boot**

Welsh
Words are usually stressed on the penultimate syllable.

c	as **k** in **king**, never as **s**
ch	as **ch** in Scottish **loch**
dd	as **th** in **then**
f	as **v** in **vine**
ff	as **f** in **fine**
ll	as **hl**, the **h** aspirated quite forcefully
rh	as **hr**, the **h** aspirated quite forcefully
w	as **w** in **wine** or as **oo** in **boot**
ae, ei, eu	as **i** in **fire**
aw	as **ow** in **town**
oe	as **oy** in **toy**
u	as **i** in **thin** or **ee** in **see**
y	as **u** in **fun**, or **i** in **thin**, or **ee** in **see**

PRIMARY SOURCES

· · · · · · · · · · · ·

Carmichael, Alexander, *Carmina Gadelica Hymns and Incantations*. Floris Books, Edinburgh, 1992

Cross, T.P. and C.H. Slover, *Ancient Irish Tales*. Barnes and Noble, New York, 1969.

Gantz, Jeffrey, *Early Irish Myths and Sagas*. Penguin, London and New York, 1981.

Gantz, Jeffrey, *The Mabinogion*. Penguin, Harmondsworth and New York, 1976.

Jackson K.H., *A Celtic Miscellany*. Penguin, Harmondsworth and New York, 1971.

Kinsella, Thomas, *The Tain*. Oxford University Press, London and New York, 1970.

FURTHER READING

Backhouse, Janet,
The Lindisfarne Gospels.
British Library Press,
London, 1995.

Bain, George, *Celtic Art:*
Methods of Construction.
McClellan, Glasgow, 1951.

Chadwick, Nora, *The Druids.*
University of Wales Press,
Cardiff, 1997.

Clancy, Thomas, and Gilbert
Markus, eds. and trans.,
Iona: The Earliest Poetry of a
Celtic Monastery. Edinburgh
University Press, Edinburgh,
1995.

Curtin, Jeremiah, *Myths and*
Folk Tales of Ireland.
Dover Publications,
New York, 1975.

Dillon, Myles, and Nora
Chadwick, *The Celtic Realms.*
Cardinal, London, 1973.

Eluere, Christine, *The Celts:*
First Masters of Europe.
Thames & Hudson,
London, 1992; Abrams,
New York, 1993.

Green, Miranda, *Exploring the*
World of the Druids. Thames
& Hudson, London and
New York, 1997.

Green, Miranda, *Dictionary of*
Celtic Myth and Legend.
Thames & Hudson, London
and New York, 1997.

Green, Miranda, *Celtic*
Goddesses: Warriors, Virgins
and Mothers. British Museum
Press, London, 1995.

Hyde, Douglas, *Beside the Fire:*
Irish Folktales. Irish Academy
Press, Dublin, 1978.

Jacobs, Joseph, *Celtic Fairy Tales.*
Bracken, London, 1991.

Joyce, P.W., *Old Celtic Romances.*
Talbot Press, Dublin, 1961.

Lover, Samuel, and T. Crofton
Croker, *Ireland: Myths and*
Legends. Senate, London,
1995.

MacCana, Proinseas,
Celtic Mythology. Newnes,
Middlesex, 1983.

Piggott, Stewart, *The Druids.*
Thames & Hudson, London
and New York, 1985.

O'hOgain, Daithi, *The Sacred*
Isle: Belief and Religion in
Pre-Christian Ireland. Boydell
Press, Woodbridge, 1999.

Raftery, Barry, *Pagan Celtic*
Ireland: The Enigma of the
Iron Age. Thames & Hudson,
London and New York, 1997.

Rees, Alwyn and Brinley,
Celtic Heritage. Thames &
Hudson, London and New
York, 1961.

Ross, Anne, *Pagan Celtic Britain:*
Studies in Iconography and
Tradition. Constable,
London, 1992.

Sharkey, John, *Celtic Mysteries.*
Thames & Hudson, London
and New York, 1975.

Stead, I.M., J.B. Bourke and
D. Bothwell, *Lindow Man:*
The Body in the Bog. British
Museum Publications,
London, 1986.

Thomas, Charles, *Celtic Britain.*
Thames & Hudson, London
and New York, 1997.

Zaczek, Iain, *Chronicles of*
the Celts. Past Times,
London, 1996.

INDEX

Cairbre, chief bard to the
Tuatha De Danann 122
calendar, the Celtic year 25–9
Canu Heledd (*Song of Heledd*)
23, 95
Caradawg Stout-Arm (Welsh) 75
Carmichael, Alexander 41
Carrawburgh (Northumberland)
77
carynx, Celtic war trumpet 15,
134
Cathbad [kaTHvath] (Irish
druid) 100–101
cauldron 78–9, *78*, 128
Ceridwen (Welsh) 86, 102–3
Cernunnos 28, *29*, 55–6
charms *34*, 116, 118
see also talismans
children, the wise child 10–11
Christ, symbolism in Celtic art
126
Christianity, assimilation of
pagan elements 37, 56, 58, 97,
101
Ciaran, St (Irish) 101
Cicero, Divitiacus and 99
cockerels, significance of 57
Collen, St (Welsh) 51–2
Columba, St 101, 113
Conaire, [konneera] High King
of Ireland 20
Conan (Irish hero) 128
Conchobar (Conor) [konchovar,
konnor], King of Ulster 16,
100–101
Conn, High King of Tara 65
Conor *see* Conchobar
Cormac, King of Tara (Irish
hero) 76, 79–81
corpse candles *21*

corrigans, Breton fairies 117
cosmic order, in Ireland 64
Coventina, well of 77
Cruachan 67, 128
Cuchulainn [koo-choolin] (Irish
hero) 12, 14, 15, 57, 100
sickness of 118–19
Culhwch (Welsh) 48
Culhwch and Olwen (Welsh tale)
55
cup, of truth 78, 81
curraghs 68
cycle of life 17, 133
Cynddylan, King (Welsh) 23, 95

D
Dagda, the 60, 78, 83
Dallan (Irish druid) 101
Danaan *see* Tuatha de
Danann
David of the White Rock
(Welsh harpist) *21*
dead, kingdoms of the 20–21
death 134–5
Ankou and 20
eternal life and 125, 134
portents of *21*
Deirdre of the Sorrows (Irish)
16, 100
Der Greine (Irish) 61
Dian Cecht [deean keht],
physician to the Tuatha
De Danann 116–18
Diarmid mac Cearrbheoil, Irish
High King 101
Diodorus Siculus, on druids 98
Diogenes Laertius, on Celts 134
divination 57, 98–9, *98*
see also prophecy
Divitiacus, druid and Aedui

leader 99
dogs *54*, 65
Donn (Irish lord of the dead)
20–21, 39
Donn Bo (Irish hero) 92–3
dragons 87, 126
Dream of Rhonabwy, The
58, 74–5
dreams 83, 98–9, 108–109, 110,
119
The Dream of Rhonabwy
58, 74–5
druids 37, 64, 134
divination 98–9, *98*
dreams and trances 98–9,
108–9
healing and 26, 29, 116, 119
ogham script and 47, 101
prophets 85
shamanic 108–9
triads, use of 114–15
water and 101
wisdom of 98–101, 134

E
earth goddess 35
Edern (Welsh) 75
egg, druid's egg talisman 109
Eloi, St (Breton) 113
Elphin (Elffin) mab Gwyddno,
(Welsh) 11, 74, 75, 128
Emer [evair] (Irish) 119
Enbarr, steed of Mannanan mac
Lir 52
Epiphany, Wise Men from the
East 45
Essyllt (Iseult, Isolda) 12, 129
Esus, woodcutter god 29, *29*
eternity, wisdom of 125–35
Excalibur 58

ACKNOWLEDGMENTS

· · · · · · · · · · · ·

The quotations in this book have all been translated from original sources and adapted where appropriate to indicate the intention of the original work. The author and the publisher would especially like to thank Dr John MacInnes for his invaluable help.

Translated and adapted by Juliette Wood: p.19; p.23; pp.31–3 (with John MacInnes); p.74–5; pp.86–7; p.95; pp.105–7; p.115; p.123; p.127; p.129; p.133; p.135. *Translated and adapted by John MacInnes*: p.41; p.73.

Other: p.70 adapted extract from The Wooing of Etain, *A Celtic Miscellany*, translation © K.H. Jackson, 1971, courtesy of the copyright holder and Routledge Ltd, London.

The publisher would like to thank the following people, museums and photographic libraries for permission to reproduce their material. Every care has been taken to trace copyright holders. However, if we have omitted anyone we apologize, and will, if informed, make corrections in any future edition. **Page 8** Bald eagle / Robert Harding Picture Library / Ron Sandford; **14** Iron spearhead with bronze detailing, 3rd to 2nd centuries BCE / Medieval and Later Antiquities Department / British Museum; **16** Goddess with owl emerging from head, detail from gold torc, 5th century BCE / Landesmuseum fur Vor- und Frühgeschichte, Saarbrücken, Germany / AKG, London; **18** Cast bronze statue of dancing girl, 1st century BCE–1st century CE / Musée des Beaux Arts, Orleans, France / Bridgeman Art Library; **19** White marble goddess statuette, 1st century BCE / Rheinisches Landesmuseum, Germany; **22** Doonagore, County Clare, Ireland / Simon Marsden Archives / Bridgeman Art Library; **24** Monastery and sacred site of Dun Conor, Inishman, Aran Islands, County Donegal, Ireland, 6th–8th centuries CE / Robert Harding Picture Library; **26** Bronze statuette of goddess Artio with bear, Stefan Rebsamen / Bernisches Historisches Museum, Switzerland; **30** Nant Bochlwyd, Snowdonia, Wales / Mick Sharp Photography; **36** Bronze boar statuette, 1st century BCE / British Museum / Werner Forman Archive; **32** Moon over sea, Getty One / Chad Ehlers; **42** Sunset over beach at Dinas Dinelle, Gwynedd, Wales, Mick Sharp Photography / Jean

Williamson; **44** Gold boat, 1st century BCE, National Museum of Ireland, Dublin / Werner Forman Archive; **49** Detail from 13th-century manuscript, British Library (Harl. 4751 folio 69); **53** Bronze enamelled dragon brooch, 1st century CE / Medieval and Later Antiquities Department / British Museum; **54** Miniature glass dog, 2nd century BCE, Landesmuseum Mainz, Germany; **62** Bardesey Island, Trwyn Maen Melyn, Gwynedd, Wales / Mick Sharp Photography; **72** Isle of Rhum, Scotland / Scottish Highlands Photo Library; **76** Gallo-Roman, wooden votive offering, 1st century CE / Musée Archéologique, Dijon, France / AKG, London; **78** Bronze cult wagon, known as "Strettweg chariot", Hallstatt period, 7th century BCE / Landes-museum Johanneum, Graz, Austria / AKG, London; **84** Lake landscape / R. Valentine Atkinson Photography; **93** Inlaid silver and niello crozier from Clonmacnoise, County Offaly, Ireland, 11th–15th centuries / National Museum of Ireland; **94** Mt Stackpolly, Rosshire, Scottish Highlands, The Stockmarket; **96** Oak tree grove, Wistman's Wood, Dartmoor, Devon, England, Sarah Boait; **104** Ruins of Tintagel, Cornwall, England, Skyscan; **111** Detail of tricephalic deity on pot, Bibliothèque Nationale de France, Paris; **112** Bell shrine of St Patrick, 12th century / National Museum of Ireland, Dublin; **124** St Agnes Beach, Isles of Scilly / F. Gibson; **132** Celtic cross, Corbis / Galen Rowell; **134** Marble statue of dying Gaul, Roman / Museo Capitolino, Rome / AKG, London.